MASTERING THE DARK ART OF REAL BARBECUE

www.heatandsmoke.com

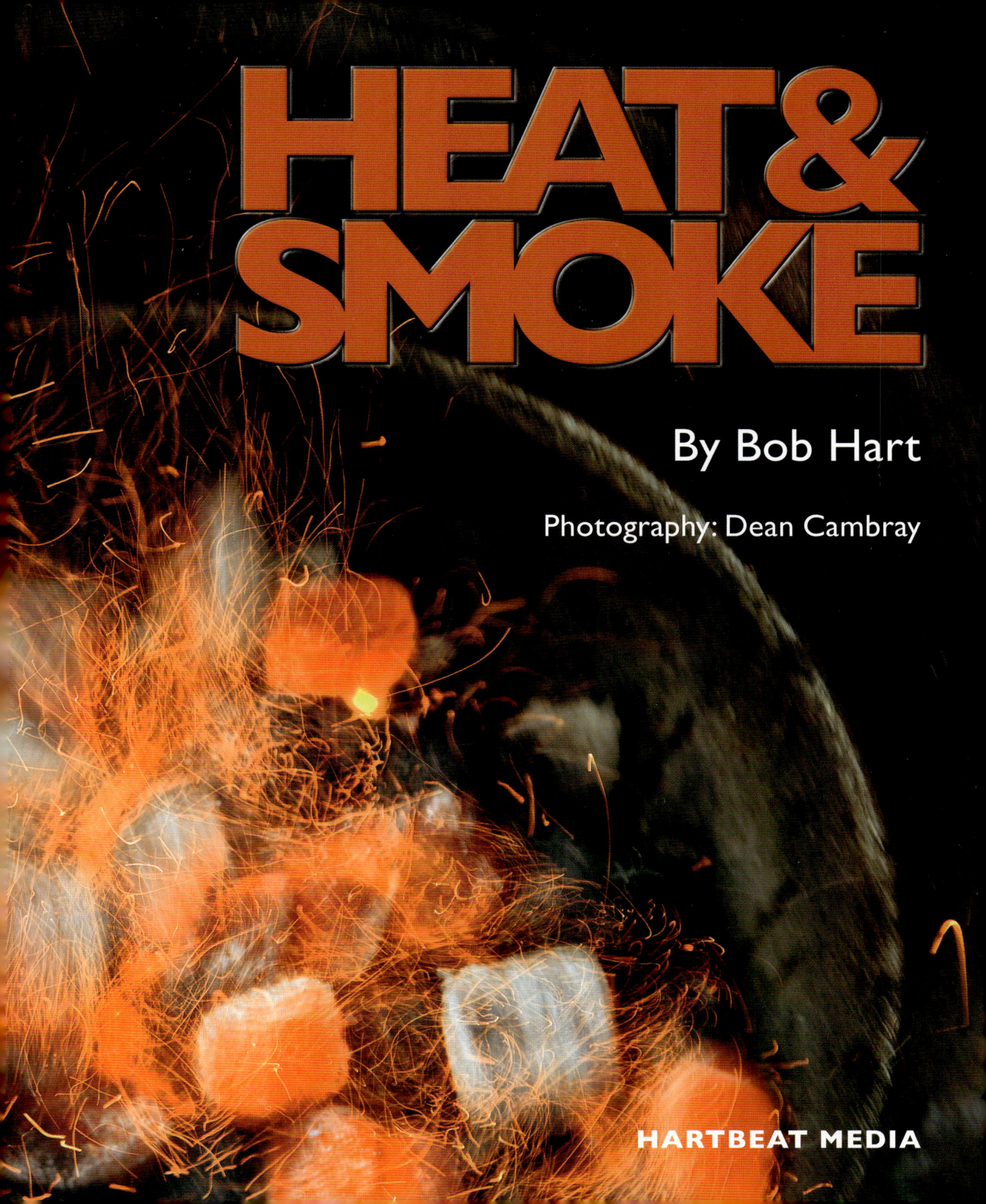

'Barbecue is the enlightened application of heat, smoke, spices and ingenuity to protein, fruit and vegetables… out of doors.'

– Bob Hart

CONTENTS

LET THE FLAMES BEGIN 1

WAYS & MEANS 2

TAKING CARE 7

RUBS, DIPS, SAUCES 11

LIQUID ASSETS 18

A CHEESE TWIST 20

SEAFOOD 26

MEAT 54

VEGETABLES 96

FRUIT 108

ACKNOWLEDGEMENTS 119

INDEX 120

LET THE FLAMES BEGIN

Welcome to a hot and smoky world of glorious aromas, incomparable flavours and food cooked expertly, and out of doors.

Welcome, that is, to the dark art of real barbecue.

The word "barbecue" derives from *barbacoa*, which means "sacred fire pit" in the language of the Taíno people of the Caribbean. They use it to describe a grill for cooking meat. But why it was ever considered sacred, unless the meat was originally sliced from sacrificial goats or slow-moving missionaries, I have no idea.

Both the word and the cooking method moved from the Caribbean into Spanish, then French, and finally English. The *Oxford English Dictionary* credits the first recorded use of the word in English, in 1697, to buccaneer William Dampier, who, being a Pom, probably over-cooked and under-seasoned the meat in question. As most of his compatriots, and many of mine, do to this day.

Barbecue is a gloriously versatile word. In most of the United States it is used as a noun to describe slow-cooked, smoked pork, generally chopped or pulled apart and eaten on a bun with coleslaw; while in Texas, it applies to an assortment of meats, the principle one being brisket of beef, cooked in much the same way as the pork but sliced rather than chopped.

In Australia, it is used (and abused) as a noun and a verb. The noun can describe the device on which meat is cooked, and occasionally cremated, or an event at which such cooking is done. The verb describes the act of cooking out of doors on a barbecue – an act usually performed, badly, by men.

Now, let's be honest: we like to think of Australia as a barbecue nation, but we are nothing of the sort. We have never fully grasped either the possibilities or the subtleties of this dark art, and the output from the average Aussie barbie is, more often than not, appalling. Improving, certainly, but still appalling much of the time. As, indeed, are many of the barbecues from which it emerges.

Americans, on the other hand, are the masters. They understand what I will attempt to convey to you through this book: that to barbecue effectively, you must apply both heat and smoke to ingredients in a way that enhances them, through flavour and tenderness, considerably; and that without both heat and smoke, it is just not barbecue. Simple as that.

I will not provide an endless stream of fiddly recipes, sooky things, or 101 ways to grill tedious stuff on sticks. Because in reality, there are only a few recipes you will ever need for each main ingredient to make your mark as a grillmaster, and I will detail these for you. Each technique I will outline will have, as you will quickly discover, multiple applications. And if you seriously want to know how to cook beef wellington on a barbecue, then this, sadly, is not the book for you.

I will cover the essential types of barbecue devices, necessary pieces of equipment, rubs, marinades, sauces and anything else that will make your life easier and more delicious. And of course, I will discuss cuts of meat, and which ones work best. I will tell you everything you need to know, but I won't waste your time.

And just so you know we mean business, every picture in this book was taken of hot, freshly prepared (by me) food, straight off the grill or out of the smoker. No stylist was used, and no jiggery or even pokery was entered into.

And that's all because I love to barbecue. And the book's brilliant photographer, Dean Cambray, and I love to eat expertly barbecued food. In fact, we like to eat. Period.

And remember: when it comes to achieving barbecue mastery, all you need is love, and a never-ending soundtrack of decent country music.

And charcoal, or maybe a gas bottle. And a few hickory chips. And a sharp knife and a pair of tongs. And a splash or two of extra virgin olive oil. And the heart of a lion. And this book, of course.

May the smoke be with you.
Bob Hart

WAYS AND MEANS: first, fire up your grill

Barbecue obsessives – and, yes, guilty as charged, Your Honour – can rattle on for days and possibly years about the merits and deficiencies of various types of barbecue. But for now, some basic information is all you should have to suffer through.

This book works on the assumption you have access to a gas barbecue – perhaps a Weber Q of one size or another, or a console barbecue like the Weber Genesis, or one of those deceptively branded, Chinese-made variations which may or may not last quite as long. Or perhaps a charcoal-fired device such as a Weber kettle – pound-for-pound the best barbecue on the planet. Or, ideally, one of each. Except for the Chinese one, that is. Which, if you already have one, will soon be rusted away beyond salvation, in any case.

There are parts of the world – Texas, for example – where these very different types of cooking devices simply do not exist in any sort of harmony. Texas barbecue enthusiasts insist that charcoal – deep, slow-burning mountains of it, smoked up with chunks of wet mesquite – is the only way to go: anything less is blasphemy.

Now if, like most Texans, your idea of the perfect barbecue is a brisket of beef, cooked for at least half a day, then this is entirely correct. In fact, my advice to you, should you even run into a Texan with a head full of mesquite smoke, is to agree with anything they tell you relating to barbecue. Then make your excuses and run for your life.

In most parts of the world, however, gas and charcoal co-exist. There is a healthy rivalry in some quarters, certainly. But the reality is that both have their strengths, and the best way to take advantage of these complementary strengths is to ensure you have access to both cooking methods.

For example, there is no more effective way to cook a steak than on a fiercely hot gas barbecue. I am lucky enough to own a venerable Weber Genesis, and a complete set of Weber Qs – a 120, a 220 and a 300. And I demonstrate this to my own, deep satisfaction on a very regular basis.

But I also have a couple of kettles, a brilliant little Weber Go-Anywhere charcoal barbecue and an incomparable Weber Smokey Mountain. In addition to a deeply loved Big Green Egg ceramic barbecue, a brilliant device, and an ornery, off-set barrel smoker to hide behind when Texans come to visit.

My assortment of gas bottles, therefore, is rivalled only by the mountain of charcoal and charcoal briquettes in my back yard. Not to mention the pile of wood chips and chunks – the chips for immediate smoke, the chunks for something that lasts a bit longer. And cedar planks, of course. And of all the woods available for smoking, my personal favourite is hickory – the wood of the pecan tree, incidentally – along with fruit woods, mesquite and, for at least one recipe (see entrecôte bordelaise), vine clippings.

Real barbecue is, at once, simpler than you could ever have imagined, and slightly more complicated. For example, consider this: if you have a hot plate on your barbecue, examine it closely. If it has a hole in one corner, that is good news as you can pass a rope through the hole, tie it, and use the hotplate as a makeshift anchor for a canoe, or some such thing.

If it does not have a hole, no problem: toss it in the river anyway. You do not need it. There is no reason, ever, to barbecue on a hotplate. In fact, nothing cooked on a hotplate can ever be said to have been barbecued. Before you ask me how I cook eggs, the answer is that I use a cast iron pan heated on the grill. This pan has other uses we'll get to later in the book (see entrecôte bordelaise again). But a hotplate? Get rid of it: give it to someone you really dislike.

When you barbecue food, the idea is to expose it to live fire – not to cause it to wallow in its own fat while it overcooks. If that is the way you like to cook, I suggest you do it in the kitchen, ideally in an electric frypan, and leave us alone in the backyard to get on with the serious stuff.

And another thing: if you cook over charcoal, which you almost certainly will have tried once you have worked through this book, remember to light your charcoal in charcoal starters using either a gas flame or newspapers, but never firelighters.

And yes, I know all about the claims about the modern ones being odourless. Nonsense. They are not, and they will compromise the flavour and quality of your food. But please, don't throw them in the river with the hotplates: they may kill the fish. Instead, give them to that bloke you can't stand and stuff up his roast lamb.

In this book, and in other barbecue manuals you may encounter, you will be instructed to cook food over either direct or indirect heat. What does this mean?

It's pretty simple, really: with a gas grill, direct heat involves firing up all the burners, while indirect means leaving the middle burner (or possibly two) turned off so you place a roasting joint, say, or a large fish, over that cooler section of the grill. In the case of a charcoal grill such as a Weber kettle, confine the charcoal or briquettes to the side baskets and fill the space between them with one or two aluminium drip trays, into which you can pour water to keep things moist and hold the temperature back a little.

Occasionally, you will encounter discussion of a two-zone fire, which simply means there is heat under one side of the grill but not the other. With a gas grill, this involves turning on the burners on one side of the cooking surface only. With charcoal, it means piling the fuel on one side of the kettle, and placing a foil drip tray under the other. Yes, I know that sounds like a lot of information. But once you have done these things once or twice, and tasted the results of your ingenuity, it will all become second nature.

But now, pay close attention. Because the most important thing to remember about real barbecue is that to become a grillmaster, which you will certainly do if you work methodically through this book, you do not need to develop either the skills or the arrogance of a chef. In fact, too many cheffy qualities can get in the way of promoting a natural talent for barbecue.

we grillmasters like to break as many of the rules followed by proper chefs as we can, as you will discover from this book. Our aim is simplicity and accessibility, not culinary virtuosity, which includes, but is not limited to, sublime knife skills.

Developing a range of real barbecue skills will afford you great pleasure, not to mention infinite bragging rights. It may even attract marriage proposals, or something similar, which may or may not be a bad thing. Also, you will look unspeakably cool at all times, which is desirable.

But always remember: real barbecue is fun, and the food it produces is simple and delicious. Pay attention, and you will never again embarrass yourself with an overcooked cutlet, a charred sausage, a blackened chicken or a fish that looks as though it has been the victim of a serious traffic accident.

Because life, I reckon, is far too short for that sort of thing. And for hotplates and firelighters. And for trying to cook beef wellington on a bloody barbecue.

NOTE: And no, since you ask, I am not sponsored by Weber. The excellence of these American-made, ingeniously designed barbecues is such that Weber simply do not need to sponsor people like me: they already know that, quite simply, I cannot live without them, and will encourage fellow enthusiasts to use their products wherever possible.

They are, however, as far as I can tell, fine people, those Weber folk. I will continue to buy and use their barbecues, and suggest you do so, also. And yes, I know they make hotplates and recommend firelighters and have even produced a tired old book that includes a recipe for beef wellington.

All of which just goes to show: nobody's perfect. Not even me.

TAKING CARE: all you need to know

When you suddenly develop an interest in the dark art of barbecue, family members may decide all of their questions relating to convenient and inexpensive gift-giving have been answered, as far as you're concerned.

And before you know it, you will be knee-deep in barbecue accessories which, frankly, you will never need. So this is as good a time as any to clear that up. In fact, perhaps you should copy this bit, and circulate to family members and close friends. Because...

To barbecue expertly, whether over gas or charcoal, there are very few essential tools.

Just these:

A couple of barbecue mitts or leather gauntlets are pretty important, especially for when you lift the entire body off the Smokey Mountain to freshen up the hickory and/or the charcoal. This is not a job to address bare-handed. Also, when you are working for any length of time over a hot grill – turning cutlets, mussels or oysters, for example – you will find a mitt or a glove to be a vital piece of tackle. It is also important, as I will remind you from time to time, for a grillmaster to look cool at all times. And there are few cooler pieces of barbecue tackle than a pair of black, suede gauntlets, monogrammed or not. Wear a pair of these, and you will really look the part: no one will doubt, especially not you, that your food is going to be sublime.

Another essential tool is a pair of tongs. In fact, make sure you have half a dozen of these, at least. But do not buy flash tongs: the best ones – the easiest and lightest to use, and the only ones that lock tight, which is important – are the cheapest Chinese aluminium varieties, the sort that cost about $5 for a couple of pairs in the supermarket. Or even less in the Asian market. Forget about stainless steel models, or rubber-covered ones, or any that look in the least bit flash. The cheap ones, quite simply, work best. And a long pair of these, you will find, is ideal for manipulating burning charcoal (while wearing a gauntlet, of course).

Tongs are also essential when it comes to preparing your grill, which is when you will also need another barbecue essential – a good, clean, wire brush. Weber make triangular ones that last longer than most, but there are several varieties on the market that work just as well. Ensure you have one to hand at all times.

Clearly essential, and undeniably cool, is an instant-read digital meat thermometer. You will be using one of these constantly when you cook larger cuts of meat, so buy a decent one. The folding probe-style one is probably the easiest to use – mine is a Maverick, and it has never let me down – although the remote version with a probe you leave in the meat also does a good job.

The advantage of the folding version, however, is that there is no better tool than one of these for lifting the membrane from the back of your rack of pork spare-ribs. Strange, but true.

And also very cool, of course.

Finally, there are various flash spatulas sold by barbecue shops, but none of them are much good. Instead, buy a paint scraper with a large blade. But remember to keep it purely for barbecue duties – lifting and turning food on the grill and occasionally scraping the grill – and do not use it for scraping paint between meals.

So, now that you have the essential ingredients – as well, perhaps, as an apron, but ideally not one with plastic breasts attached to the front: black and sturdy is just fine – you can make a start on the routine through which you should run whenever you are about to start grilling.

The object is to ensure your grill is clean, hot and oiled at all times: so make that your mantra. First, clean your grill thoroughly with a wire brush, then light the gas and drop the hood for about 10 minutes if you are cooking over gas, or allow your charcoal to become evenly white and very hot before covering the kettle for a few minutes, and then oil the grill.

To do this, convert a paper kitchen towel into a small square by folding it four times. Clamp this square in your tongs, dip it into a bowl of oil – I always use an extra virgin olive oil, simply because I see no point in owning more than one oil which will serve all purposes – which you should keep by your grill at all times. Brush this over the grill to coat it, and you will see flames rise from the heat bars or charcoal as some of the oil drops through. Which will tell you, as if you didn't know already, that you are ready to rock. And possibly roll. But certainly to grill.

And while this is all you have to know about preparing your grill before cooking on it, there is something else you need to know: never, ever wash a cast iron grill in detergent. It will destroy the excellent cooking surface you are working so hard to develop, and food will be more likely to stick.

This is less of an issue with stainless steel, obviously. But while I will happily use a steel pad on a stainless steel grill, I never apply detergent. Don't ask me why, because I don't really know: I just don't do it.

So now, let's fire up a grill or two, send up some smoke, annoy the neighbours and cook stuff, shall we?

RUBS, DIPS, SAUCES: where less is more

Entire books, and probably rooms, have been filled with recipes for these vital components of barbecue mastery. But frankly, life is too short to read them all, let alone make most of them.

Each may well have something distinctive to recommend it. But, essentially, you need to focus on creating a quantity of an all-purpose dry rub in which you have faith, and a large jar of basic barbecue sauce.

I have tried most recipes for these, and I have settled on a versatile rub which links, effectively, to a simple but delicious uncooked barbecue sauce.

You will find these, along with a couple of things such as mop sauces for slow-cooked beef or pork that I also use, to be more than adequate for most barbecue adventures.

And if you stumble upon another component that you find especially attractive, as you almost certainly will, simply add it to your repertoire. Because the sauces, rubs and techniques you discover for yourself may, ultimately, be the ones that give you the greatest satisfaction.

But start by making quantities of these two – a dry rub, a barbecue sauce and a couple of other odds and ends that slot right in with my approach – and store them in suitable, airtight, non-reactive containers.

The barbecue sauce should probably be refrigerated, and will keep for several months. The rub will also keep for at least that long, but may lose some of its intensity. But the rest should be made as you need them which, in the case of the chipotle mayo, for example, will probably be most days.

But then, if you are hovering around the barbecue and sending up smoke as often as I expect you to be after you have eaten your way through this book, none of this will be a problem.

an all-purpose dry rub ...

This rub, pictured left, will work on pork, chicken, beef and just about anything else you cook with heat and smoke. Combine 1 tbs dry mustard, 1 tbs sweet paprika, 1 tbs dark brown sugar, 1½ tsp garlic powder, 1½ tsp onion powder, 1½ tsp celery salt, 1 tsp cayenne pepper, ½ tsp ground allspice. This makes a single quantity but, frankly, I suggest you start by quadrupling it!

chimichurri ...

The magical Argentine sauce, chimichurri – a fiery variation of salsa verde – is another great way to breathe new life into grilled meat, chicken or fish. The spice takes care of the smoke and the vinegar cuts through the richness. Prepare it as you need it, although it will hold in the fridge for a week or so. Some of the ready-made bottled versions are, frankly, pretty good. But try making your own first.

Pick about four cups of parsley leaves and one of fresh oregano. Put them in a food processor and purée with 5 large garlic cloves, three-quarters of a cup of EV olive oil, half a cup of white wine vinegar, a splash of sherry vinegar and a good splash of water, half to one teaspoon of dried, hot red chilli flakes, sea salt and freshly ground black pepper to taste. For a variation, use two-and-a-half cups of parsley, one of coriander leaves and half a cup of mint leaves.

You can use some of the sauce to marinate, for about an hour, sliced and flattened slices of scotch fillet for a dish called churrasco. Sear the slices briefly over charcoal or on a hot grill, with hickory smoke, and serve with more fresh chimichurri. Alternatively, spread a whole or part of a scotch fillet with chimichurri, roast by the indirect method, again with hickory smoke, to achieve an interior temperature of 45-50°C. Rest it for 20 mins under "tented" (loosely covered) foil in a warm place, slice it and serve with plenty of chimichurri.

north carolina vinegar sauce (for pork) ...

This thin sauce is essential for slow-cooked, chopped pork shoulder to which the sauce is added before it is served on a hamburger bun with coleslaw. To make it, mix 2 tbs brown sugar, 4 tsp sea salt and 3 tbs tomato ketchup into 2 cups cider vinegar. Add 1 tsp Tabasco and, if you like it as fiery as I do, 1 tsp chilli flakes and a few grinds of fresh black pepper.

mint pesto ...

Process 50g of blanched, raw almonds to a paste with a well-packed half cup of fresh mint leaves, 2 peeled cloves of garlic, a pinch of salt, ¾ cup (or even a bit more) of EV olive oil and a dash of sherry vinegar. Stir in 40g of parmesan (Italian - grated on a microplane for lightness). And that's it.

compound butters ...

The use of carefully and freshly prepared compound butters, I have found, is the best way, by far, to add a highly distinctive character to certain grilled offerings. I use a parsley compound butter for steak or large, grilled mushrooms, a dill butter for salmon with chipotle as an option, a tarragon butter for grilled chicken, with basil as an option, and so on.

To make these butters, simply bring 125g of unsalted butter to room temperature and add 1 tbs of dijon mustard, 3 small or 2 large cloves of minced garlic, a squeeze of lemon and 2 tbs of the fresh herb you are using or, in the case of a chipotle butter, 2 chopped chipotle chillies in adobo (tinned) and 1 tsp of the adobo sauce. Mash these mixtures together and place each on a square of plastic wrap. Roll them into sausage shapes, twisting the ends closed, and then wrap them again in foil,

CHIMICHURRI

MINT PESTO

VINEGAR SAUCE (PORK)

PARSLEY BUTTER

BARBECUE SAUCE

twisting them closed. Place them in the freezer to set. To use them, slice off discs of the compound butter and serve them on top of the hot, grilled dish. In the case of the mushroom burger, let the butter melt into the gills while the mushroom is still on the grill and, for the steak sanger, soften enough compound butter to spread on the bottom of each ciabatta roll as well as topping each piece of steak with a disc.

an all-purpose barbecue sauce...

This sauce, pictured on the previous page, locks in with the rub you have just made. Mix 1½ cups tomato sauce with ¼ cup molasses, ¼ cup cider vinegar, ¼ cup water, a splash of liquid smoke and whisk in 2 tbs of the rub mixture. At this point I also add a splash of bourbon, but please yourself. It is worth making this sauce your own by adding an ingredient that you believe adds to it. For me, it's bourbon. But for you it may be rum, grappa, Milo, chipotle powder or whatever ticks your boxes. When you are happy with your sauce, bottle some up for friends, but never EVER tell them what's in it. Lie, if you have to...

the chipotle mayo miracle...

When someone uses the word "miraculous" in food circles these days, they are probably about to tell you about a Mexican product called chipotle (pronounced: chip-oat-lay) chillies — dried, smoked jalapeños. They are excellent in dried form, often sold ground as a fiery powder, but the best way to buy them is as tinned, whole chillies or peppers, reconstituted in a tomato-based sauce called adobo. Buy a case of small tins of these just as soon as you have finished reading this, and your life will improve.

Chipotle mayonnaise, pictured right, has an infinite number of delicious applications — as a dip for grilled vegetables as well as a spread for grilled meat sandwiches or for life-altering burgers and mushroom sangers. So open a tin, remove four whole chillies, remove any stem ends and finely chop the whole chillies, seeds and all. Add them, with a spoonful or two of the adobo sauce, to 8-10 tbs bottled mayo, such as Best Foods or Hellmann's. Add 2 tbs of sour cream and combine. Store this, covered and refrigerated, in a non-reactive container. And if, for any reason, you find this mixture a bit fierce, simply reduce the heat by adding more mayo and sour cream. Or if you want heat, more chillies and adobo sauce. You are in charge here.

And remember, you will seldom use a whole tin of chillies at a time. So rather than sitting that half-empty tin in the back of your fridge until it grows whiskers, tip the contents into a small freezer bag, remove the air and freeze it. When next you need to make chipotle mayo, simply take it out of the freezer, remove it from the bag and grate as much as you need on a coarse microplane grater.

salsa verde ...

Salsa verde is a glorious green sauce – brilliant on all grilled meats, fish and even vegies. I especially like it on a quickly grilled slab of white fish – oiled, seasoned and cooked skin-side down on a hot gas grill (covered, of course), and never turned – such as a fillet of blue-eye or rockling. But frankly, it adds magic to just about everything. The recipe is traditional, but is not etched in stone. Play with the sauce if you like, but before you do, try this classic version: combine, in a food processor, 2 handfuls of picked, flat-leaf parsley with a handful of basil leaves and another of mint. Add 2 tbs of capers, four cornichons (small gherkins), 6-8 anchovy fillets, 1 tbs dijon mustard, 3 tbs red wine vinegar and a splash of sherry vinegar, a cup of your finest EV olive oil and black pepper. Season to taste with salt, but be careful as the anchovies may deliver enough salt. Also, add extra oil if you think it needs it.

mop sauce (for beef) ...

When a brisket of beef, rather than a pork shoulder, is luxuriating in the smoker, mix a cup of distilled white vinegar with a cup of beer. Add 1 tbs garlic salt, 1 tbs brown sugar, 1 tsp chilli flakes, 1 tsp freshly ground black pepper and a good dollop of tomato ketchup. Apply this every hour for the first four or five hours of cooking.

RUBS, DIPS, SAUCES

mop sauce (for pork) ...

Slow-cooking/hot smoking joints of meat like beef briskets or pork shoulders means you need to work on the meat to maintain a suitable moisture content. The way to do that is with a mop sauce, sloshed over the meat, with a mop or silicon brush, every hour or so for the first four or five hours. To make a typical mop sauce for pork, add 1 tbs sea salt and 1 tsp freshly ground pepper to 2 cups white malt vinegar. Add 1 tsp dried chilli flakes and 1 thinly sliced onion. Do not start applying this sauce to cooking meats until the outside is well sealed. Then, mop away.

remember ...

While I have provided basic recipes for these vital aspects of barbecue, they are purely recommendations. To extract maximum satisfaction from the process, it is important to add your own distinctive touches to all of these things. So if you think rubs should contain ground coffee and/or dried chipotle, and that barbecue sauces should contain chocolate and/or vodka, and that compound butters should contain hundreds-and-thousands, nothing should stop you from trying those modifications for yourself. With the possible exception of the hundreds-and-thousands, OK?

But first, let's pour a couple of drinks...

RUBS, DIPS, SAUCES

LIQUID ASSETS: cut through the smoke

The ideal opening lubricant for any barbecue assembly is (a) a very cold beer or five or (b) a glorious and refreshing concoction called lime moscato (pictured) – an incomparable drop on a hot summer's day.

LIME MOSCATO:

6-8 LIMES

2 BOTTLES OF MOSCATO

HOMEMADE LEMONADE:

3 LARGE LEMONS (ZEST)

250G WHITE SUGAR

250ML LEMON JUICE

FRESH MINT

LEMON SLICES

Make it by chilling, in a tall jug, the juice of 6-8 limes. To this, add two very cold bottles of moscato. I used the delicious Brown Brothers version – great drinking at under $20.

I also make jugs of lemonade, as a non-alcoholic pipe opener, as follows: warm 250ml water. Add 250g white sugar and zest of 3 large lemons. Stir until sugar dissolves and boil for 30 secs. Cool to room temperature, add 250ml lemon juice, seeds removed, and briefly return to boil. Add handful of fresh mint leaves and allow to cool. Strain and bottle. Dilute with iced water or sparkling mineral water, to taste, and serve with lemon slices and mint sprigs.

But all of that is, of course, just for starters. And for fun. Beer and cider are fine accompaniments for smoky, barbecued food, as is a crisp Australian riesling, such as any of the better ones from the Clare Valley, followed by a sturdy red, such as an Australian shiraz, a shiraz-viognier, a GSM or a straight grenache.

Or, for the genuine barbecue aficionado, anything carrying the glorious Victorian label, Ladies Who Shoot Their Lunch, especially the acclaimed shiraz. These wines are not simply outstanding, they are made by a team who understand barbecue. Which, so often, points to an insistence upon excellence, right?

No sooky, over-wooded chardies or wimpy, girly pinots, please, when there is hickory smoke in the air. An earthy and substantial pinot, however – perhaps a Kiwi one, or a top one from the Mornington Peninsula, or Beechworth, or Gippsland, but don't expect a good one to be cheap – is hard to beat with a rotisseried duck or char-grilled duck breasts (page 94).

A CHEESE TWIST: making a start

Cheese, more often than not, is something that comes late in a meal, and not at the beginning. But barbecue offers a world of difference in so many ways, and this is one of them.

WHITE MOULD CHEESE

FRESH GARLIC

RED WINE

FRESH THYME

BAGUETTE

Because when friends gather around a barbecue in anticipation of a serious meal, it is important to begin with something that sets the scene. And, frankly, nothing does this job and delivers a welcome more effectively than a white mould cheese, gently roasted in its own wooden box.

Try this:

Buy any good, white mould cheese presented in a circular, wooden box. My favourites include a French triple-brie called a Clarines, or the Old Telegraph Road cheese from Jindi Cheese in Gippsland. Also, any good French camembert will do the job, and deliver a ton of flavour.

To prepare the cheese, remove the lid and, if there is one, the plastic film over the cheese, slice a couple of cloves of fresh garlic into spiked chards and press them into the surface of the cheese. Sit the box on a square of foil and wrap it so that the foil comes about 1cm up the sides of the box, making a seal. Pour a couple of glugs of red wine onto the cheese and pop a sprig or two of fresh thyme on top.

Now, place the cheese, on a trivet, in the middle of a hot grill and forget about it for about 15 minutes, or until it starts to froth on top. Remove it from the grill and let it rest for just long enough for you either to cut a fresh baguette into spikes, or even cut one, at a shallow angle, into oval slices which you can quickly grill before plunging them into the cheese and surprising even yourself.

HALLOUMI: another hot cheese option

Even if you happen to be Greek, halloumi (or haloumi) cheese may not the first ingredient you think of when you fire up the barbecue. But perhaps it should be.

2 RED CAPSICUMS
2 COBS OF CORN
LEMON
2 CURED CHORIZOS
4 TBS EV OLIVE OIL
1 TBS SHERRY VINEGAR
SMOKED PAPRIKA
FLAT-LEAF PARSLEY
250G HALLOUMI
SALT
CHILLI FLAKES
BROAD BEANS

Because as the key ingredient of a very lively salad that slots comfortably into any barbecue banquet, ideally at the beginning, this pale cheese is a winner.

Try this:

Fire up a hooded gas grill and, on it, cook a couple of large red capsicums, turning them as they blacken, for up to 20 minutes.

Lift them off and drop them into a large bowl. Cover the bowl with plastic wrap and let them sweat for 10 minutes or so.

While that is happening, dry-roast a couple of cobs of fresh corn, following the approach outlined on page 100. Slice the roasted kernels from the cobs and put into a serving bowl.

Now, peel the blackened skin from the capsicums, halve and deseed them and slice them into strips. Add to the corn.

Grill two lightly oiled, cured chorizos (sausages), sliced, at an angle, into (roughly) 8mm slices, until they are cooked through, and some nice, dark grill marks have appeared. Add these to the capsicum strips and the corn, along with a generous handful of broad beans which have been cooked in boiling, salted water and double-peeled. Add 4 tbs of EV olive oil, 1 tbs of sherry vinegar, a pinch of smoked paprika and a handful of coarsely chopped flat-leaf parsley.

Finally, slice, on angle, 250g of good halloumi – the Cypriot Aphrodite Halloumi is the best I have tried – into 5mm slices, oil it lightly with EV olive oil and grill it for about a minute on each side on that same clean, oiled and very hot gas grill.

You will need a good, thin spatula (your paint scraper, OK?) to do this. Season it with salt (if necessary), chilli flakes and a squeeze of lemon. Add it to the rest of the ingredients and toss gently to combine. Serve immediately as a first course or part of that barbecue feast, or as an opulent side dish.

JALAPEÑO POPPERS: the friendly fire

These glorious chillies (or peppers) are a backbone ingredient of modern barbecue. They are the soul of chipotle mayo – chipotle are dried, smoked jalapeños – to which you will be addicted by the time you have worked your way through this book.

12 GREEN JALAPEÑOS

CREAM CHEESE

HAM OR COOKED PRAWNS

DRY-CURED STREAKY BACON

But fresh jalapeños – readily available, even in some supermarkets – are brilliant grill fodder in a dish called jalapeño poppers, perhaps the greatest barbecue appetisers of them all.

Try this:

Buy a dozen of the largest green jalapeños you can find – big fat ones, like a very large man's, um, finger. Split them, from the top downwards, but leaving them joined at the bottom (stem) end with the stem attached.

Scrape out the seeds and white pith: I use the spoon end of a lobster pick for this, but any small spoon will do. Go about this carefully and do it thoroughly as it is the seeds and the pith that carry the excess heat in these chillies.

Now, make a stuffing, and use your imagination. Mash some cream cheese at room temperature. Stud it with pretty much anything you like – finely chopped ham or cooked prawns, perhaps. But whatever you use (it is a chance to put your signature on a barbecue offering: if you want to use finely cubed pineapple, do so), you roll the finished cheese into bullet shapes to fit neatly into the split chillies, and squeeze them closed.

Take a thin rasher of dry-cured streaky bacon for each chilli and carefully wrap it in a spiral. Some people skewer this in place and, if you do, use a small metal skewer rather than a wooden one as even soaked skewers catch fire. But I simply leave the bacon untethered, even if it ends up falling away slightly from the chillies, and handle it carefully with tongs.

Cook the poppers on a hot gas or charcoal grill. Turn them carefully as the skin blisters. They will soon start to soften as the bacon cooks and the filling melts – at which point, lift them off the grill, on to a serving platter, and remember to let them cool slightly before popping one, or even two, into your mouth.

IN THE SWIM: seafood braves the flames

There is an assumption barbecuing involves cooking, or even over-cooking, stonking great slabs of red meat over fierce heat. Which is nonsense, of course.

Good meat, as you will discover later in this book, can be turned into something quite magical through the smoky alchemy of barbecue. But then, so can vegies, fruit and — perhaps even more memorably — seafood.

The delicacy of molluscs, crustaceans, white fish, salmon, trout, even calamari, is significantly enhanced through careful exposure to heat and smoke. But as always, there are a few things you need to know, and a few techniques to master.

For the simplest example, simply take a generous slab of sturdy white fish such as blue-eye, oil and season it as you would a steak and position it, skin side down, on a very hot barbecue. Drop the hood and leave it in peace until it is cooked through. Cooking time will vary with the size of the slab of fish and the heat of your barbecue, but 10-12 minutes should do the trick.

Check with the tip of a thin, sharp knife and, when the fish is almost cooked, you will find the skin will release from the grill, and will be crisp and delicious. Lift it off, rest it briefly to finish cooking, and serve it with a generous dollop of salsa verde (page 16). Got the picture?

But that is seafood barbecue in its most basic form. There are other, even more exciting miracles to perform.

So fire up the grill, pick up those tongs, and hold on to your hat, Algernon.

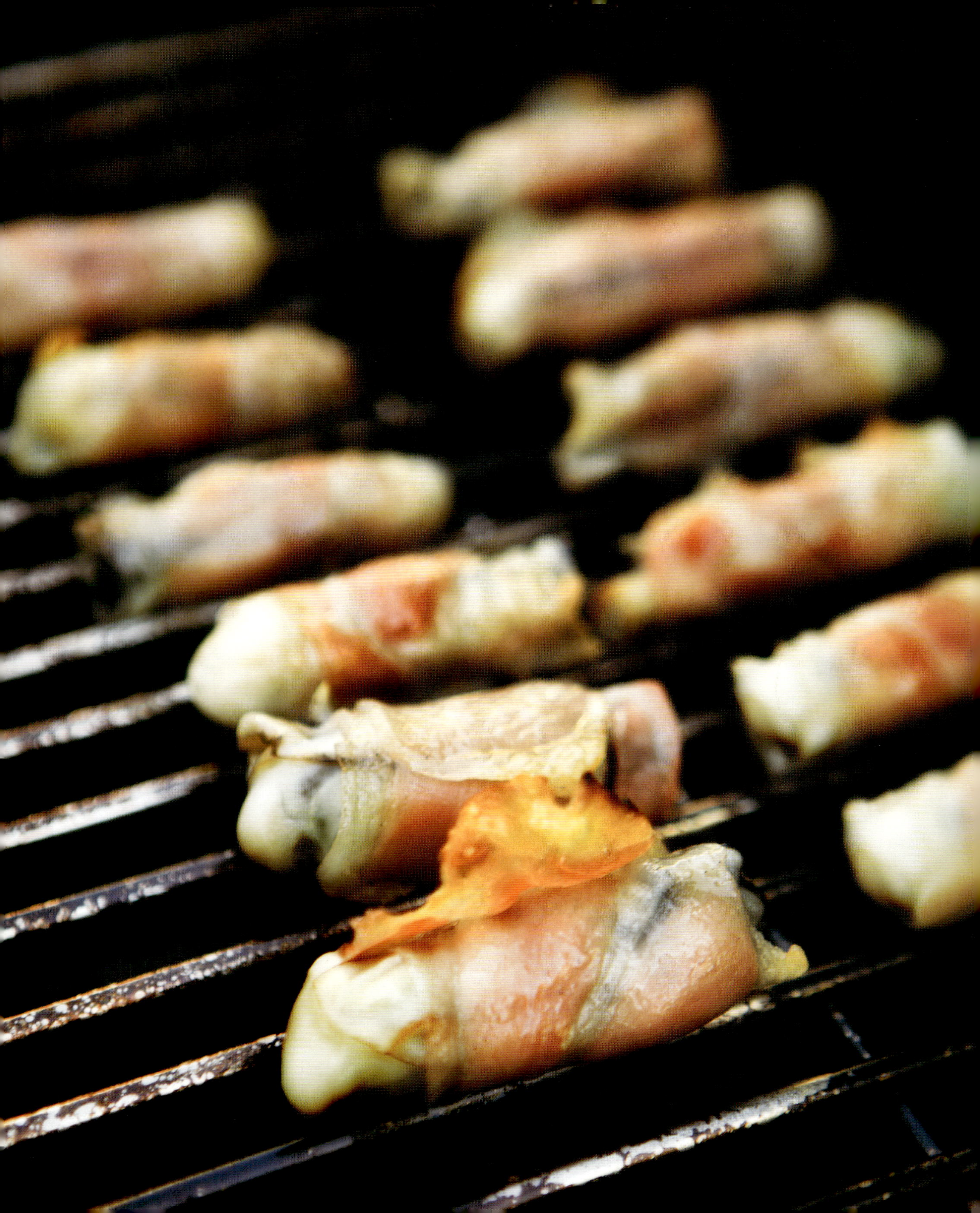

OYSTERS: where the mollusc meets the smoke

Oysters, which strike me as an ideal ingredient with which to begin our exploration of barbecuing seafood, are among the most distinguished and delectable of all sea creatures – unless you are a member of the unhappy band of eaters who find them unpalatable.

If you are, there is little more I can tell you. But if the very thought of oysters – whether fresh and cold with the tang of the sea, or cooked in the way I am about to outline – makes your pulses race, then read on.

FRESH OYSTERS
PROSCIUTTO
SEA SALT (TO SERVE)

When oysters are at their best, there is no doubt the best way to eat them is as God intended – freshly shucked, detached from their shells and then poured, straight from those shells and with their own juices, down your throat. Heaven.

Variety, however, still spices our lives as effectively as ever and, with that in mind, I strongly advise you try a batch of oysters prepared, over direct heat, on your barbecue. The larger Pacific oysters are ideal for this dish.

Either a gas or charcoal barbecue will do the trick. My preference is for charcoal – again, so the oysters can go through the cooking process swathed in sweet wood smoke. Hickory is fine.

So, fire up a Weber kettle or a Big Green Egg set up for direct grilling. Place a trivet – Weber make particularly good ones, large and small, from stainless steel rods – over the centre of the grill. If you are using a gas grill, go for maximum heat and position the trivet in the same way. Then, try this:

Lift the oysters from their shells, one at a time, and position them at one end of a paper-thin slice of prosciutto. Then, roll the oyster in the prosciutto until it is neatly wrapped.

Lightly oil the trivet, and position the oysters – half a dozen makes a good single portion or, as an appetiser with drinks, two or three each may suffice, depending on what's to follow – between, and parallel to, the bars. Cover the grill.

After a minute or so, raise the hood and use small tongs to turn each oyster through about a third of a turn and, after another minute or so, turn again. When the prosciutto begins to crisp and colour and the oyster plumps up, they are ready.

KILPATRICK SAUCE:

200ML RED WINE VINEGAR

150G CASTER SUGAR

100G RED ONION

1 TSP CHILLI FLAKES

½ TSP CRACKED PEPPER

150G HORSERADISH

150ML WORCESTERSHIRE SAUCE

When you place the oysters on the grill, surround the trivet with their shells, just to warm them. And when the oysters are ready, lift the trivet off the heat and position the shells, with the use of mounds of sea salt, on a serving platter.

Into each shell, brush a smear of sauce – either the kilpatrick-style sauce outlined below, or, even more simply and in the spirit of the backyard, my "bloody mary" oyster sauce made by stirring horseradish and a dash or two of Tabasco into tomato ketchup. Arrive at your own proportions according to the strength, or otherwise, of the horseradish.

Position an oyster on the sauce in each shell and then top with a bit more of the sauce. Eat.

For the slightly more elaborate but quite delicious kilpatrick sauce, boil 200ml of red wine vinegar with 150g of caster sugar, 100g of finely chopped red onion, 1 tsp of chilli flakes and ½ tsp of cracked pepper. Reduce over medium heat and add 150g of horseradish (bottled, but not horseradish cream) and 150ml of Worcestershire sauce.

Reduce again to a thick syrup, allow to cool, and use instead of the bloody mary sauce.

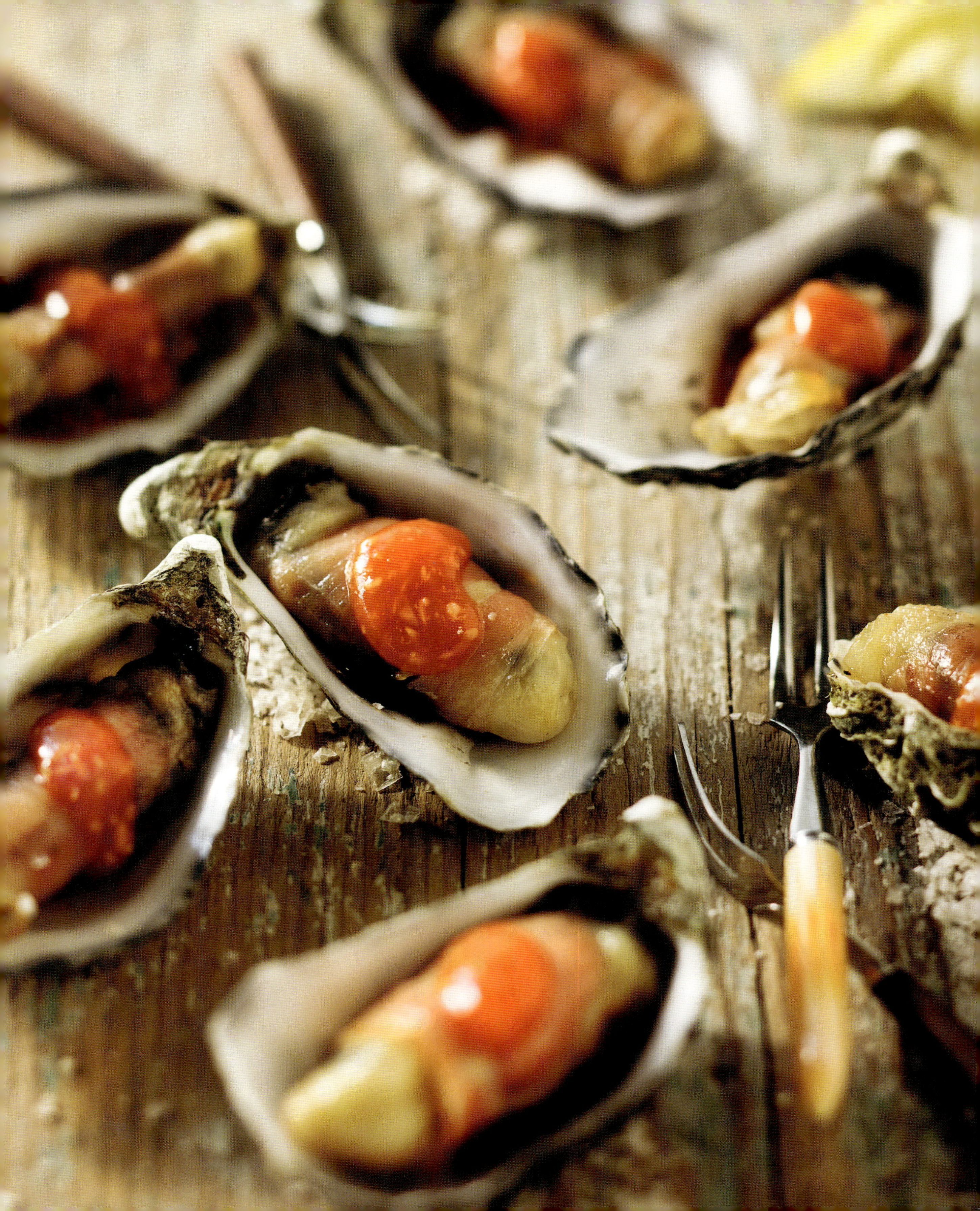

GRILLED MUSSELS: smoke on the butter

Anyone who is not seriously in love with fresh, black mussels – those glorious, modestly priced, working-class molluscs – simply needs to try harder. Or, possibly, they urgently need to toss a kilo or so of the shiny, jewel-like creatures on to a hot grill for a whole new perspective.

1KG FRESH BLACK MUSSELS

2 HALVED LEMONS

CHOPPED PARSLEY

125G UNSALTED BUTTER

MINCED GARLIC (OPTIONAL)

SEA SALT

PARSLEY BUTTER

BAGUETTE

Europeans love mussels – especially the French, the Dutch and the Belgians. There, they are usually steamed open in a covered pot with white wine, butter or oil, parsley, garlic, occasionally chilli and one or two other things. And they are delicious.

But frankly, I think my simple but spectacular grilled version – prepared quickly and simply out of doors – is even more delicious. And if you do the preparation, as I do, on a Big Green Egg or a Weber kettle and waft clouds of hickory smoke through the mussels as they are opening, you may become seriously addicted.

So, try this:

Rinse and de-beard a kilo of fresh, black mussels. Discard any that do not close when you tap or squeeze them. Spread the rest over a hot grill – it can be a gas grill but mussels are even more delicious if you cook them, over direct heat, in a charcoal barbecue to which you have added wet hickory chips.

Place a couple of lemon halves face down on the grill. On the same grill, place an oven-safe pot containing 125g of unsalted butter and a generous handful of chopped parsley and minced garlic if you like. Drop the hood or, on a kettle, replace the lid.

Check after a couple of minutes and, as the mussels open, dip them in parsley butter, into which you have squeezed some grilled lemon and added sea salt, and then toss them into a warmed bowl. Drop the barbecue lid for another minute or so and repeat until all the mussels have opened, been lifted off and buttered.

Now you could, I suppose, wait until all the mussels have been transferred to the bowl before sharing them around. But I suggest you do no such thing. Start eating them as soon as you have a batch buttered, wiping the bowl with chunks of crusty baguette. I suspect you will not stop until the mussels are finished.

After which you may notice you have a buttery mouth and have begun to speak with just the hint of a Belgian accent.

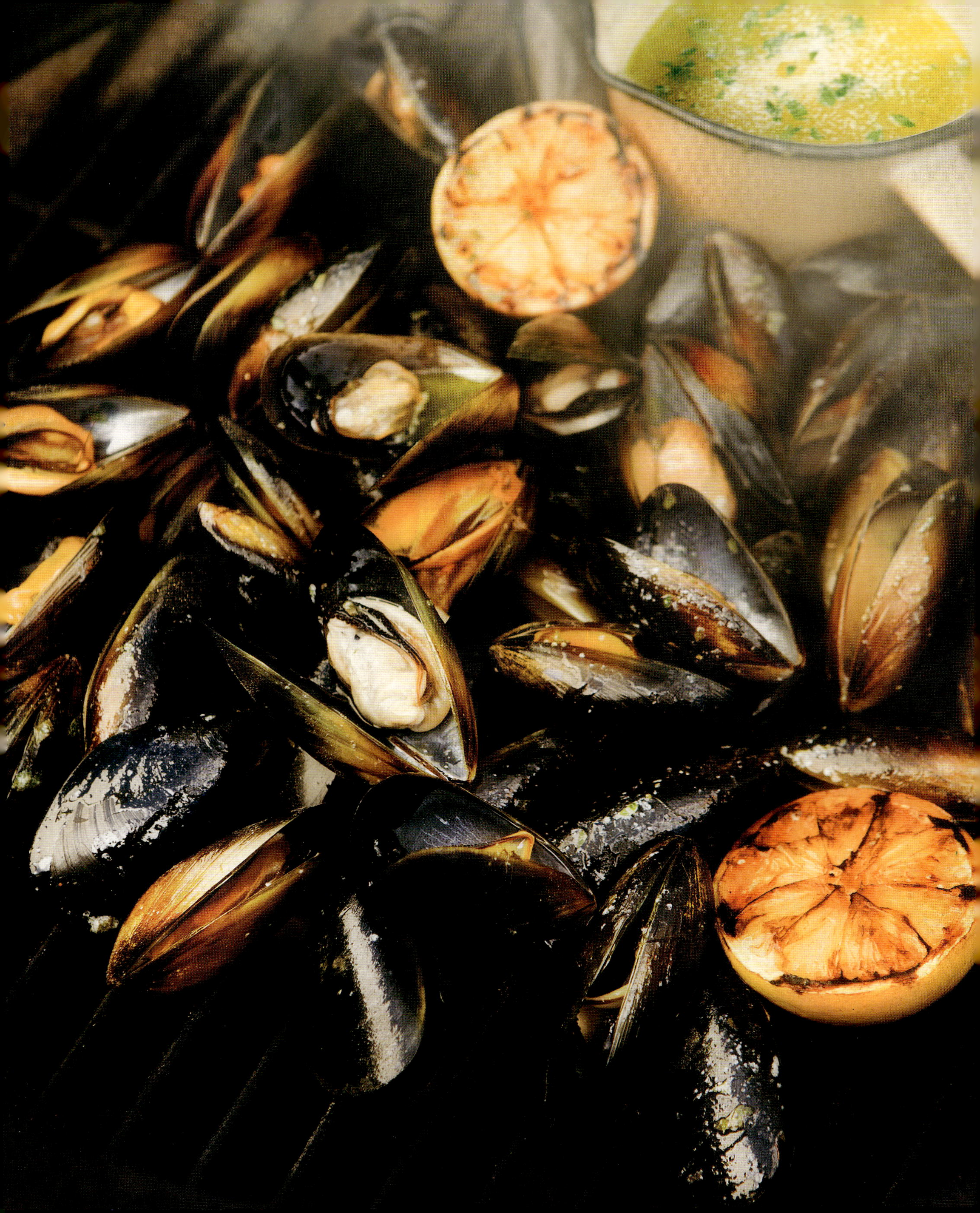

KING PRAWNS: first build a raft

King or tiger prawns – the larger the better – are fine barbecue tucker. There is any number of great and often complicated ways to prepare them, but none better than these – one moderately fiddly, one gloriously simple, both delicious.

12 LARGE KING PRAWNS

LEMONS

EV OLIVE OIL

1 FRESH CHILLI

PROSCIUTTO

For the trickiest of the methods, remove the heads from a dozen large king prawns, peel and devein them (i.e. remove the poop tube by opening them down the back with a sharp knife), but leave their tails in place. Marinate them, briefly, in the zest, flesh and juice of a lemon to which you have added a splash of olive oil and a small, hot, pounded or minced chilli.

Wrap each prawn in a strip of prosciutto, and then skewer them – three or four at a time – and make into rafts by lying them flat, parallel to each other. Use thin metal skewers – even well-soaked (in water) bamboo skewers will probably burn, but you can try them if you like – to impale each group of prawns, twice, as illustrated. This will make them easier to flip on the grill.

Prepared in this way, the prawns should be cooked quickly but briefly.

Set up your Webber kettle or Big Green Egg for direct cooking and add a few soaked hickory chips to the charcoal, or fire up your gas grill. Cook, covered, in the middle of the grill, for only a few minutes a side. Serve with a squeeze of lemon and a glass of chilled riesling.

For an even simpler approach, and my favourite way to cook prawns, simply devein them by splitting them down the back, leaving the heads and shells in place. Give them a few minutes in that same marinade (after you have performed the poop tube surgery), and then skewer them into rafts, three or four at a time.

Grill them, fast and briefly, and serve with just a squeeze of lemon. And that glass of riesling. Or possibly two.

Now, THAT'S a prawn…

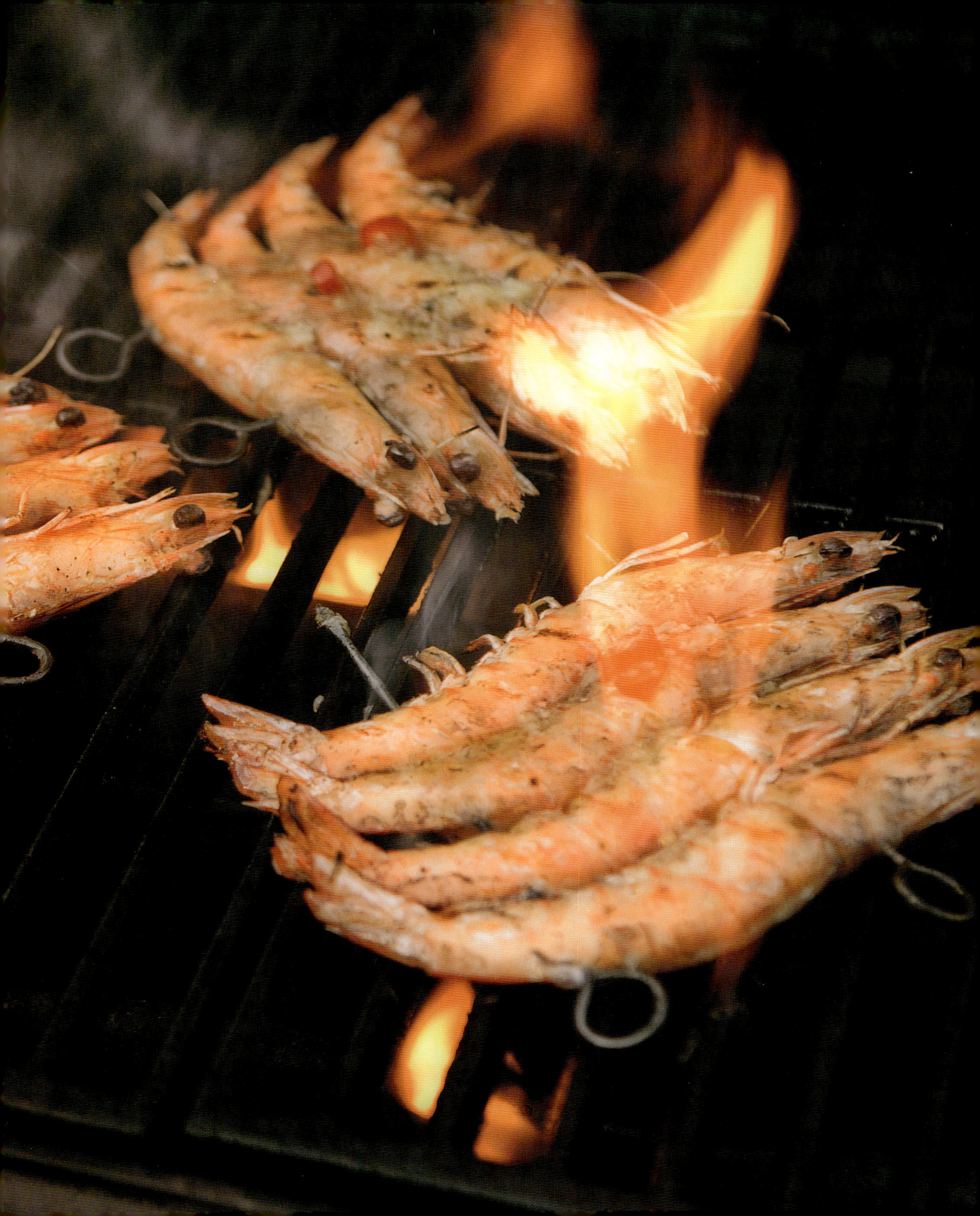

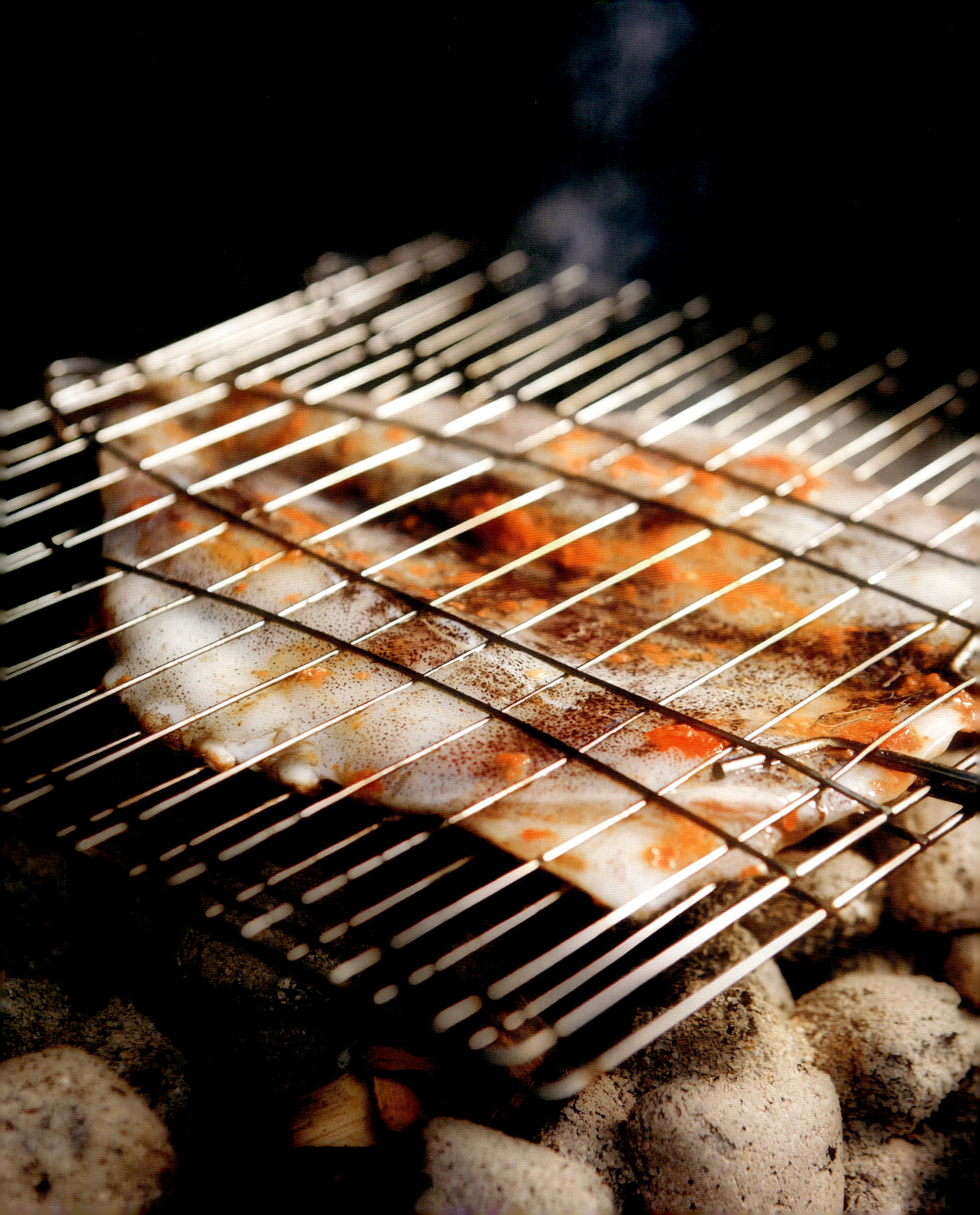

CALAMARI: the other crackling

There are a couple of questions we need to ask ourselves when we decide to make a meal of freshly caught calamari.

FRESH CALAMARI

3 RED CHILLIES

3 TBS SEA SALT

1 FRESH LIME

Should we eat the big one, or a couple of the smaller ones? Should we fire up the deep-fryer, inside, to cook salt-and-pepper squid? Or should we behave like serious grillmasters and try the Vietnamese barbecued approach?

If the squid are fresh enough, there are no wrong answers. Big or small, they are delicious. But our preference, inevitably, is always going to be for cooking out of doors over live fire.

Extreme freshness is essential: Vietnamese fishermen often carry a charcoal brazier on their boats to cook this dish minutes after hauling cephalopods aboard. This, even for me, is a step too far.

I am entranced, however, by this traditional cooking method, and by the revelation that the skin of a calamari, which most of us go to so much trouble to remove, is not unlike thin pork crackling after the squid has been quickly seared over hot charcoal. So leave it in place, and try it for yourself:

Pull the tentacles, and everything attached to them, from the squid tube of either a large, medium or small fresh calamari and put them aside to freeze for snapper bait. Without skinning the tube or removing the flaps, split it down one side and open it out flat. Remove the cartilage. And that's it.

Make a paste by pounding together, using a pestle and mortar, three fresh, small red chillies and 3 tbs of coarse sea salt. Spread both sides of the squid tube with this paste and clamp it into a flimsy, racquet-like, hinged grill. I bought mine in an Asian market for around $6.

Place this over high, direct heat, ideally from a bed of charcoal, for 3-4 minutes a side. Drop the hood – I like to cook it in a Big Green Egg or a Weber Go Anywhere – and cook a large calamari four minutes on the first side and three on the second. For a small one, three and two minutes.

Remove it from the grill, cut it into strips and serve these with a squeeze of lime. And that's it. Except, maybe, for a cold beer or three – perhaps a Vietnamese beer, out of gratitude.

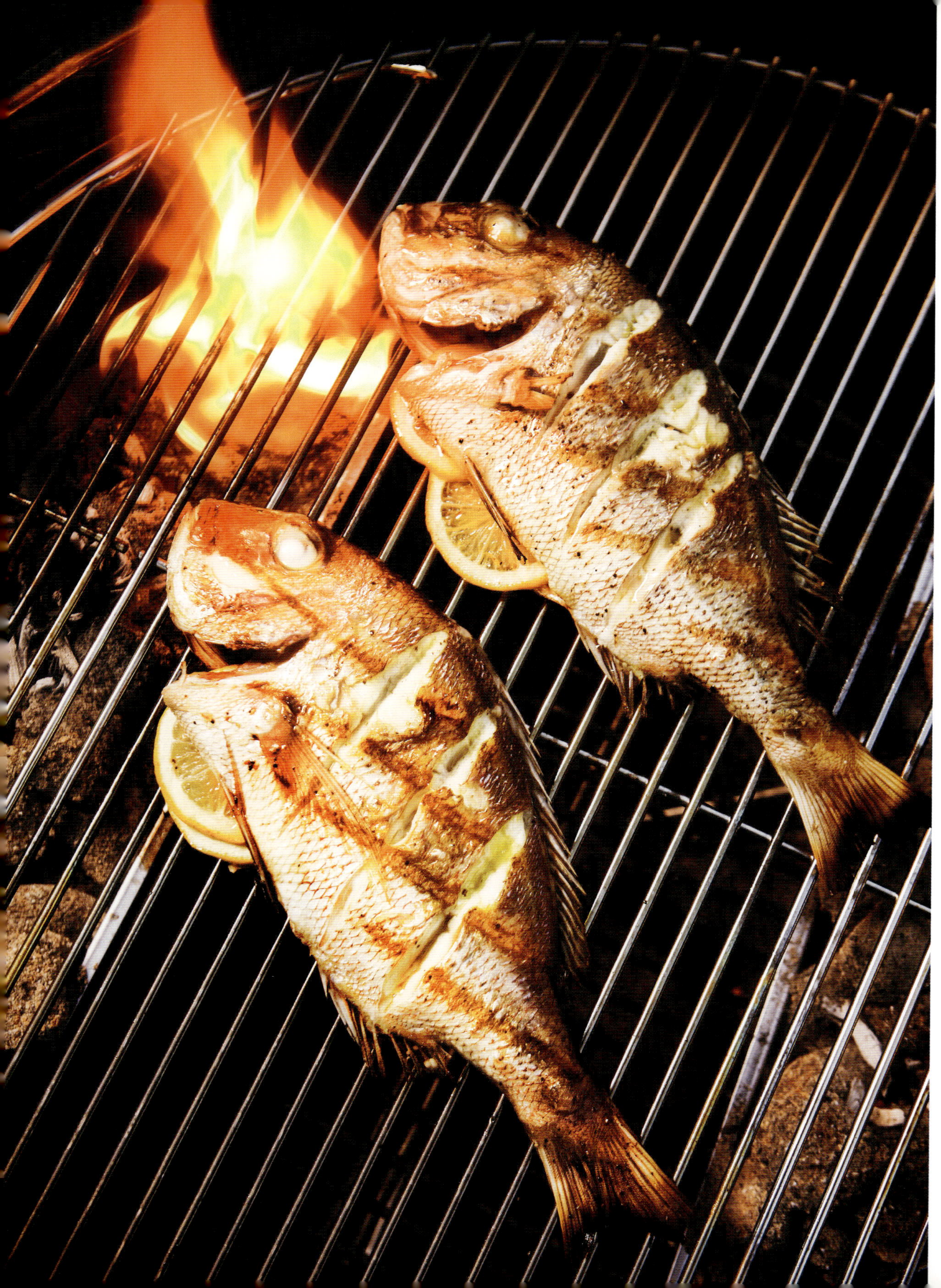

PERFECT PINKIES: by any other name

Now let's assume, just for a moment, you are someone who likes to catch their own pinkies. Or whatever it is you call infant snapper in your part of the world. Squire, perhaps?

PINKIES

EV OLIVE OIL

SALT

BLACK PEPPER

LEMON

FENNEL

But should you not only be lucky enough to be able to do this, but also prepared to cook them soon after you have done so – while they are still as stiff as boards – remember, less is more.

So when I harvest pinkies from the waters off Melbourne's Half Moon Bay – each usually around the 40cm mark and weighing about 800g – I cook them simply. Try my method – which works miracles with other small reef fish and bream, too – for yourself:

First, scale and clean the fish, remembering to remove the gills, ideally in the water in which you caught them.

Oil each fish with EV olive oil and season well with salt and freshly ground black pepper. Now, slip alternating slices of lemon and fennel into the body cavities, and cut a couple of slices through to the backbone, across both sides of each fish.

Cook the fish on a gas grill or, even better, in a Big Green Egg or even over direct heat in a Weber Kettle with some hickory smoke in the air. The fish is done when the flesh can be lifted away from the backbone, but remember: remove it from the heat before it reaches this point and rest it, loosely tented in foil, to finish cooking. The time will depend on the heat source, but around 20 minutes including a few minutes resting time will wrap things up.

One more tip: once you have placed the fish on your grill, which you have cleaned with a wire brush and then oiled, of course, leave it alone to give it time to begin to cook, and for the skin to release from the grill.

You will still not get a perfect result every time – much depends on your grill, and perfection is a crashing bore anyway, or so I am told. And a bit of torn skin adds to the authenticity. But if you are careful...

I serve fresh pinkies cooked in this way with very little else: melted butter, perhaps, into which I squeeze a little lemon juice. With a dollop of silky mash and a lightly dressed green salad on the side. And a glass or five of my favourite riesling, OK?

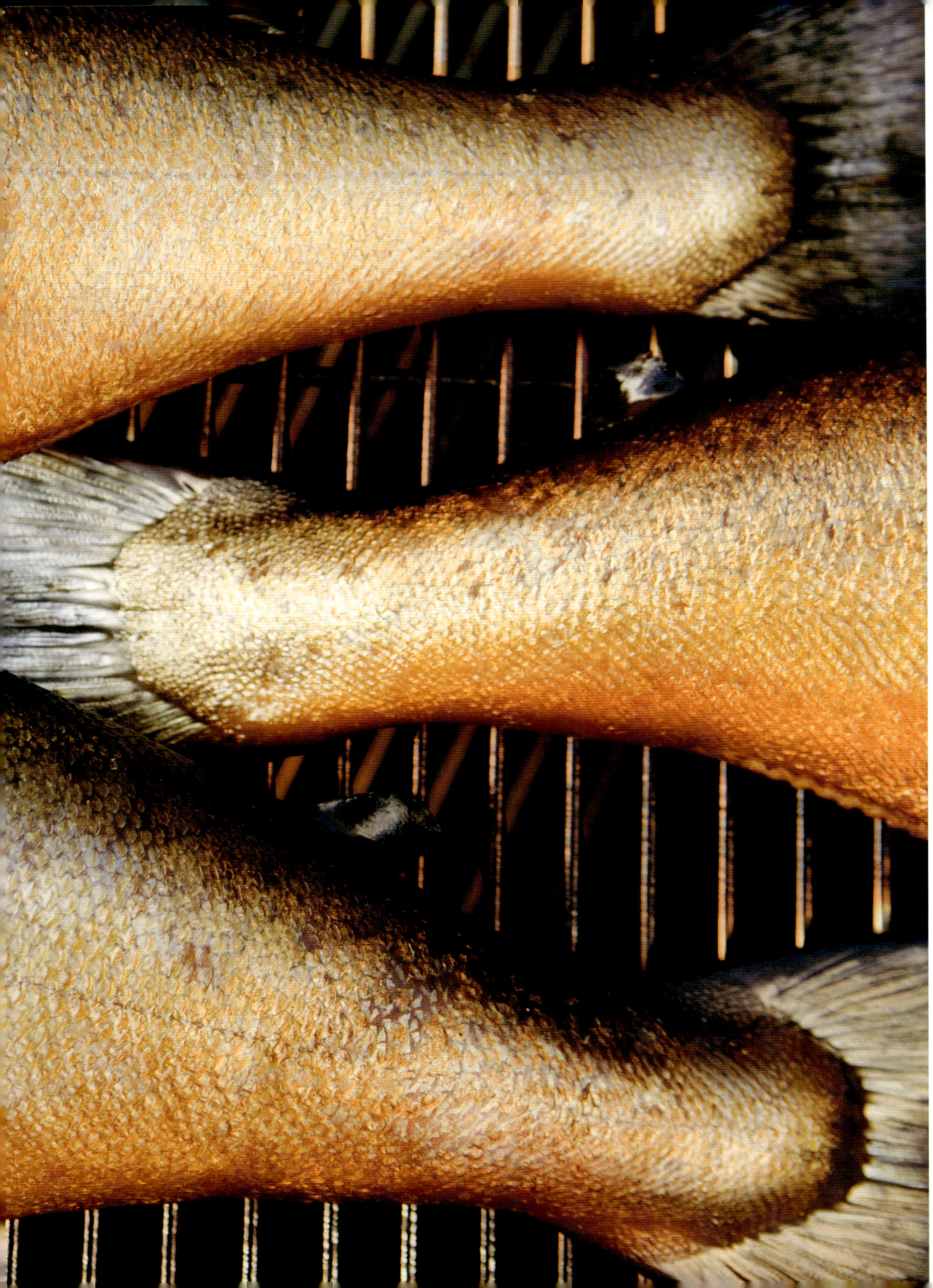

SALMON: an aristocrat among fish

Salmon – real ones, and not the undistinguished native "salmon" caught around our shores – are foreign to Australian waters. But, thanks to the miracle of modern aquaculture, they need not be foreign to our barbecues.

Try one of these noble fish cooked whole: oil and season it well, stuff it loosely with alternating slices of lemon and fennel, slash each side through to the bone in a couple of places and position it on a template of heavy card – fish shaped, but slightly smaller than the fish you are cooking, and covered with a couple of layers of heavy foil, and oiled.

Roast the fish, indirectly, carefully turning it once after about 15-10 minutes, depending upon size. Check for doneness by testing the flesh at the base of a slit, but remember to take it off before it is quite done because, like most protein, it will continue to cook.

Serve it with a drizzle of melted butter laced with chopped, fresh dill and a squeeze of lemon.

We are all spoiled rotten in terms of salmon supplies. Australia and New Zealand have booming aquaculture industries delivering fit and healthy Atlantic and Pacific salmon, pretty much all year round.

In Australia, it's Atlantic salmon or ocean trout, generally from Tasmania. Atlantic salmon are also farmed, mainly for their roe, in Victoria's Yarra Valley.

But when it comes to exposing a slab of salmon to heat & smoke, I prefer the Pacific chinook or king salmon farmed in the pristine waters off Nelson in New Zealand's South Island, and flown into Australian cities up to three times a week.

This is a terrific product – more robust and earthy than the refined Atlantic variety, and with fewer aquaculture aftertastes, I find.

Try it – oiled, seasoned and quickly grilled over direct heat, covered, skin down, not turned.

Or, better still, use it to make easily the best barbecued salmon dish of them all: planked salmon.

MORE SALMON: fish meets cedar

First, buy some cedar planks or, if you know a reliable timber merchant, untreated cedar shingles. Look at planks in a barbecue shop and trim shingles to similar proportions by lopping off a few inches from the thin end. This, ultimately, will save you a small fortune because the planks that barbecue shops import are not cheap, and this dish is addictive.

WHOLE SIDE OF SALMON

CEDAR PLANKS OR SHINGLES

EV OLIVE OIL

SEASONING

Now, try this:

Soak a plank, which will hold several fillets, in water for at least two hours, under a weight. The idea is to get it very wet so it will not catch fire, but will give off aromatic cedar essence, steam and smoke as it heats and, ultimately, scorches. Discard it after one use.

Buy a whole side of salmon: there are several recipes that will use up the off-cuts, fresh salmon keeps well for a couple of days, and it's usually cheaper by the side. Now, cut slim, centre fillets, crossways – one per person is the way to go, and you can vary the width of the slabs according to the appetites involved.

Check one fillet for size on the slab, trimming from the belly end as necessary, and then cut the other fillets to match, reserving the off-cuts. Carefully skin, oil and season the portions, and position them on the plank, crossways, or at an angle. Then, place the plank over high but indirect heat on any barbecue, and lower the hood.

There is no need for any additional wood smoke with this dish as the cedar will burn around the edges and hot-smoke the salmon in the time it takes for it to cook – 15-20 minutes, depending upon the heat of your barbecue. It will cook, all being well, before the cedar dries out and bursts into flames. But keep a spray bottle of water handy, just in case. When the salmon is cooked, carefully pull the whole plank off the grill and on to a platter, using tongs.

The flesh, cooked through, like all hot-smoked fish, will be firm but delicate with just a hint of cedar. And your backyard will smell like a sauna, which is no bad thing: it may even attract passing Fins who may well cavort naked through your geraniums, which can be diverting.

The salmon, meanwhile, will be moist enough to eat without a sauce. But a disc or two of herb butter (page 12), made with freshly picked dill, will elevate the dish in spectacular fashion.

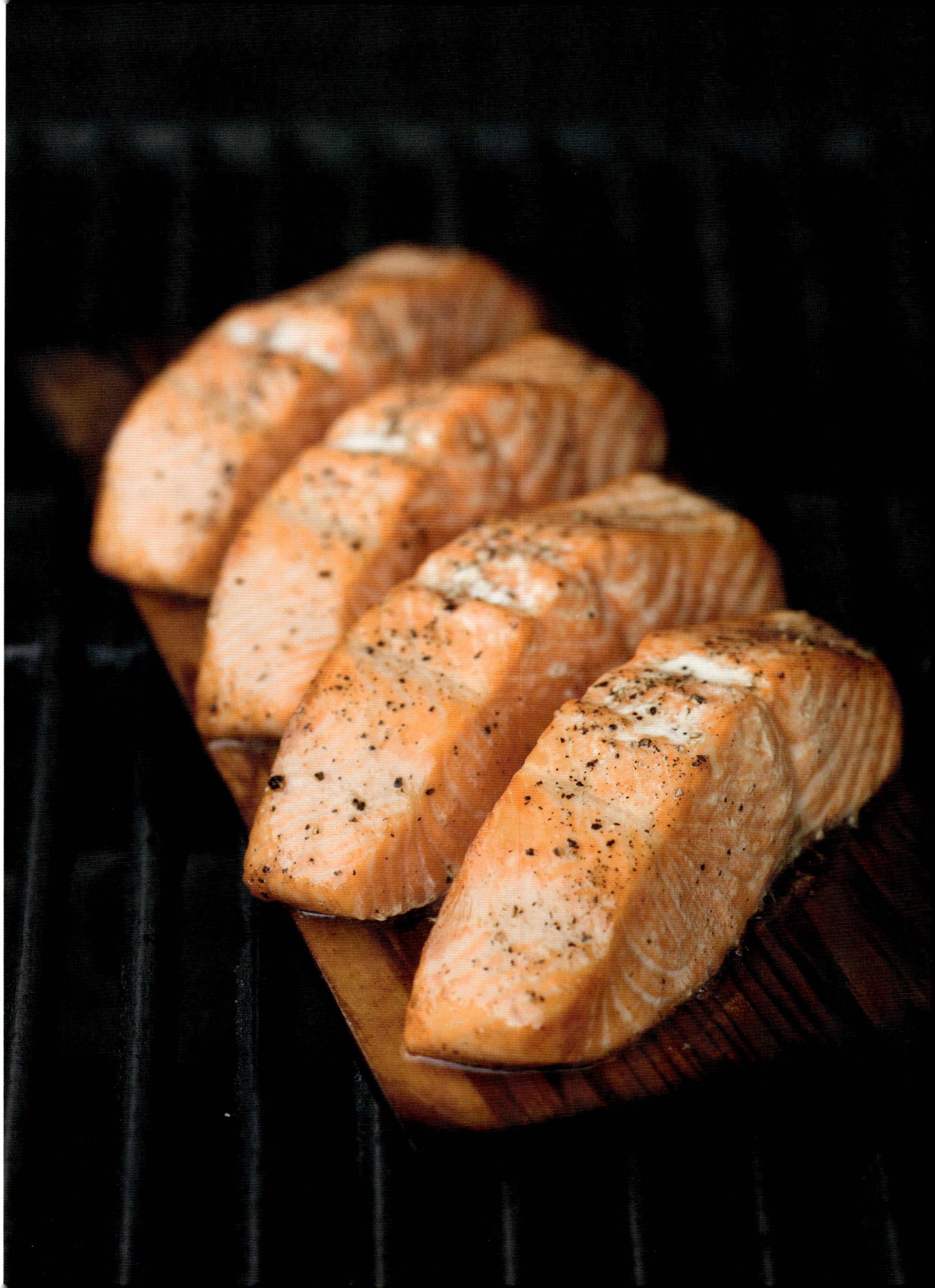

BABY SALMON: the bacon miracle

With the arrival of Chinook or King salmon into the Australian market, the game has changed. And these new products from mainly New Zealand producers include some rippers.

BABY SALMON
DRY-CURED BACON
SEASONING
BUTTER (MELTED)
FRESH DILL
LEMON

The baby salmon they have introduced are especially good. They are even better if you take the trouble to wrap them in bacon before roasting them.

To do this, buy half a dozen or so long rashers of dry-cured bacon per fish – the amount you need will vary according to the size of the fish, obviously.

Wrap each of the salmon (which you have seasoned inside and out), with the bacon, overlapping the rashers as illustrated, with four to six rashers, again depending on the size of the fish.

Place these over direct heat, and roast them, turning them often, until they are cooked through, and the bacon is well coloured and starting to crisp – probably for around 20 minutes.

Most barbecues will handle this dish if you think it through, but my favourite for the job is a well-damped Big Green Egg or a Weber kettle – in both cases with smoke rising from hickory chips.

Cook the fish quite gently until the bacon becomes crisp and golden – possibly around 20-30 minutes, but this will depend, as always, upon the size of the fish.

To serve, run a pair of kitchen scissors up the centre of the bacon and open it up slightly, run a blade down the centre of the fish and open it up slightly, and drizzle some melted butter, laced with fresh dill and a squeeze of lemon, over the whole thing.

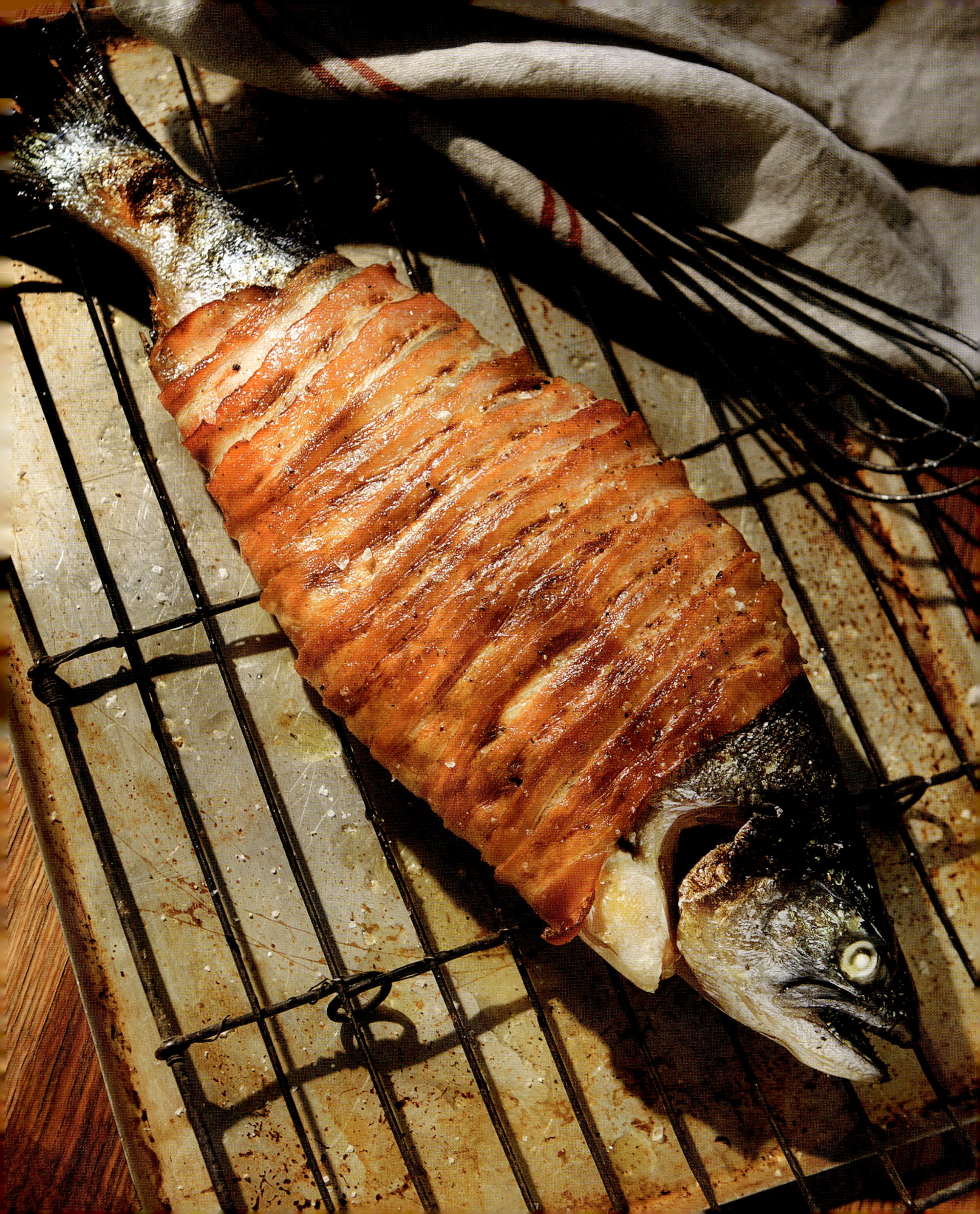

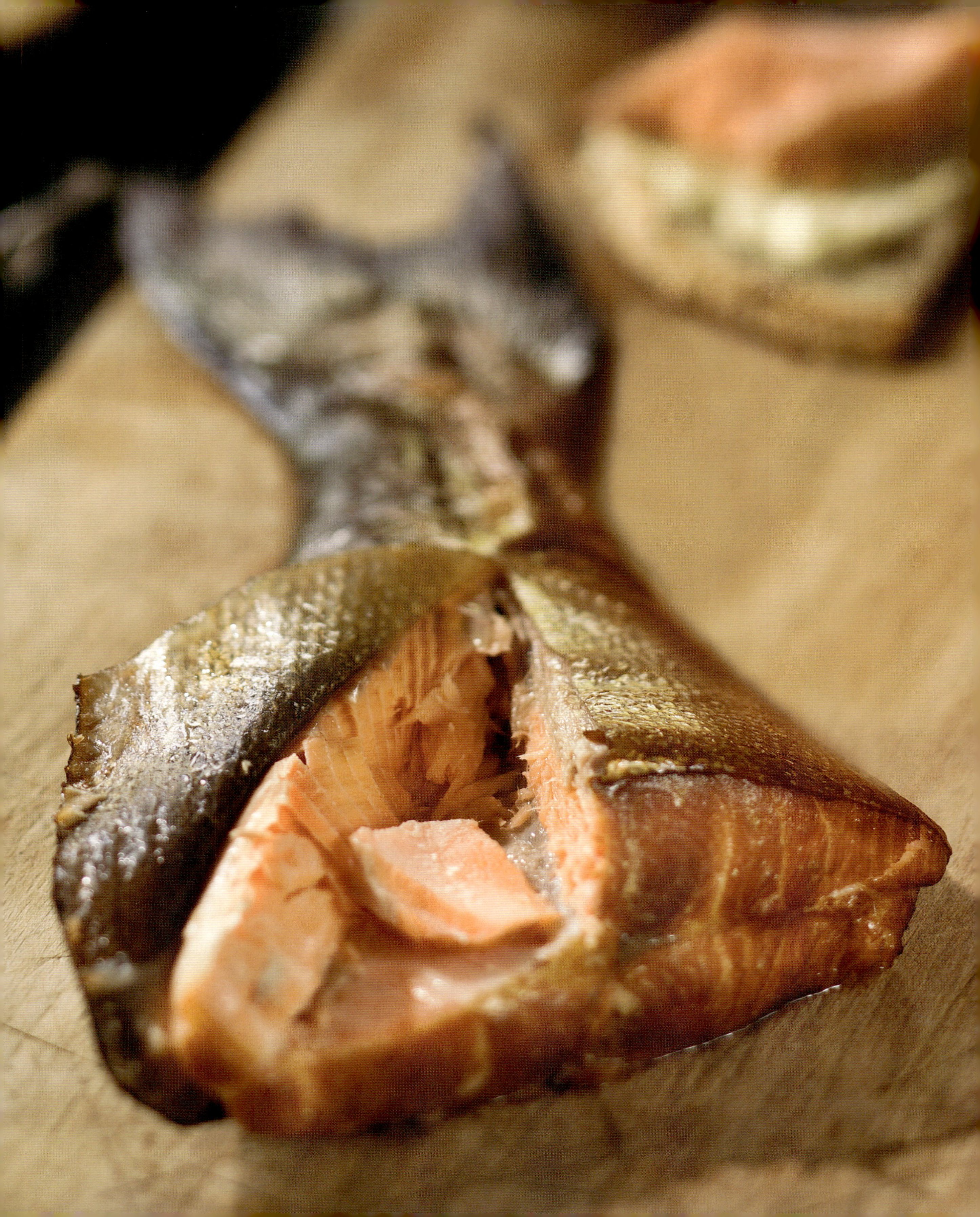

LIKELY TAILS: hot smoked salmon

The tails of large salmon are a curious by-product of this same booming market for Kiwi salmon steaks or darnes. These steaks simply become too small once they are cut from below the stomach cavity, and the alert salmon producers have now recognised this, and delivered a brilliant new product – those sturdy tails – to market.

SALMON TAILS

3 CUPS OF SEA SALT

3 CUPS OF BROWN SUGAR

LEMON

FRESH GINGER

There is no better way to cook these than to hot smoke them, ideally in a Weber Smokey Mountain. I like to brine them for at least four hours. For four of them, dissolve 3 cups of sea salt and 3 cups of brown sugar in 3 litres of water. Add a sliced lemon and about 8cm of fresh ginger, also sliced. Brine the tails in this solution for about four hours before smoking.

Place the salmon on an oiled grill in your smoker or, better still, hang them in the smoker to prevent them sticking to the grills and tearing the skin.

Smoke the tails for at least 2 hours, and up to 3, and marvel at the way, with the assistance of plenty of hickory smoke, they develop a golden hue and take on an almost jewel-like quality.

Take the tails off the smoker, let them cool to room temperature, peel back the skin and serve them with thin slices of wholegrain bread and fresh horseradish – grated and stirred into crème fraîche with a pinch of salt.

If there are any left, pop them in the fridge. They are just as good the next day and, with fresh wholegrain bread and more of that creamy horseradish, make the world's best salmon sangers.

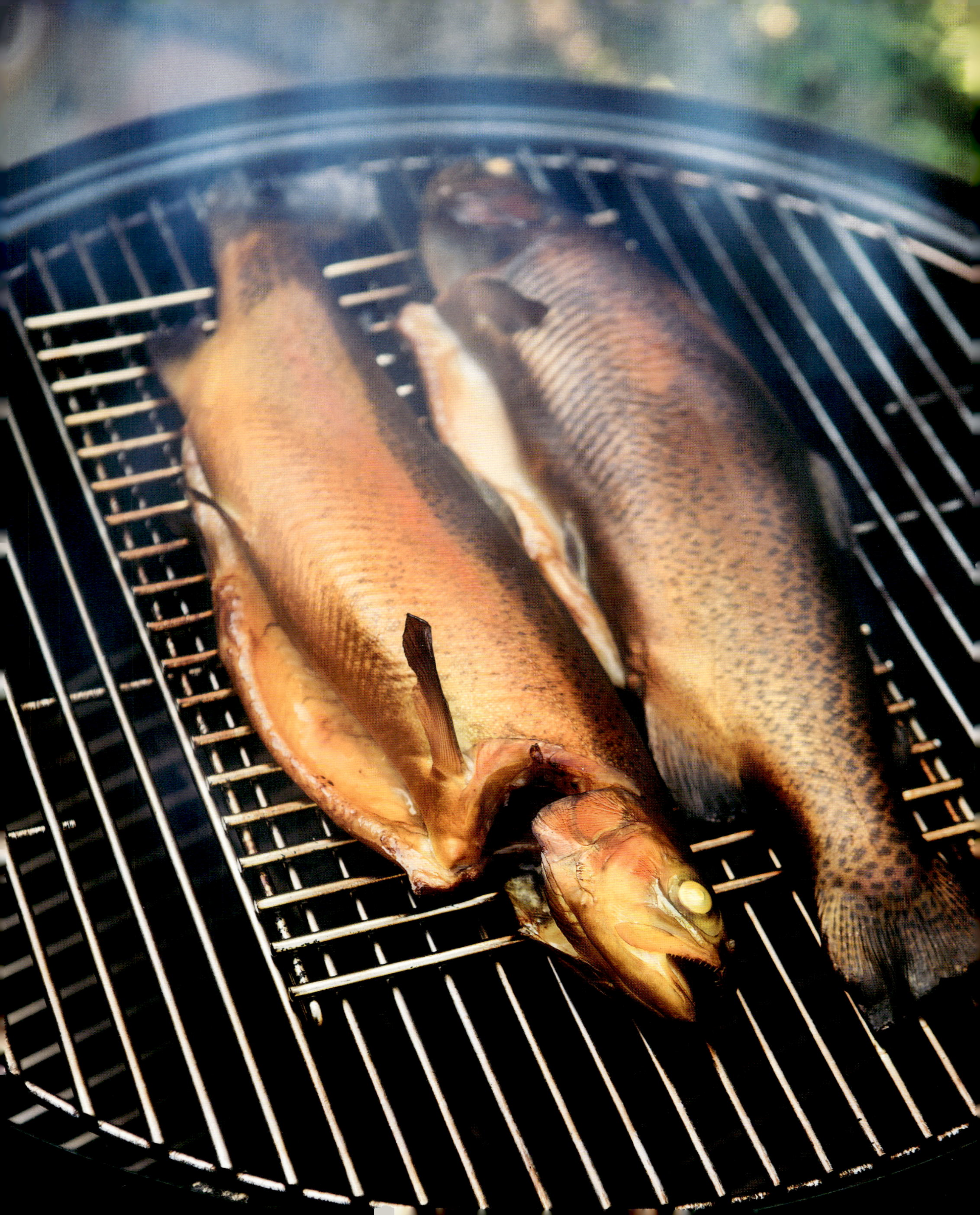

TROUT: a fish that demands respect

A trout, it is often said, is a fish far too good to catch just the once – if, indeed, you can catch it at all. This, of course, is the basis upon which fly-fishermen choose to return a trout to the pristine waters from which they have enticed it, rather than kill and eat it.

RAINBOW TROUT

½ CUP OF SEA SALT

½ CUP OF BROWN SUGAR

LEMON SLICES

FRESH GINGER

FRESH HORSERADISH

CRÉME FRAÎCHE OR SOUR CREAM

In general, I support this approach. But occasionally, I give in to temptation, and permit myself to dispatch and keep a couple of smallish fish, provided I do not have too far to walk back to camp.

There, I prepare these muscular little fish very simply – by cleaning and seasoning them, and wrapping each in one or two rashers of dry-cured, streaky bacon in much the same way I prepared the baby salmon.

But for trout, I fire up a small barbecue – the Weber Go-Anywhere charcoal grill is my preferred device for this, and something no campsite should be without – and cook them, covered, over direct heat with plenty of smoke from dampened wood gathered from the banks of the stream from which I harvested the fish. And if there is anything in the world that tastes better than that…

The approach to preparing trout I take more often, however – probably because it is not dependent on my catching a couple of the elusive little blighters and being close enough to camp to cook them immediately – is to buy a couple of trout, invariably rainbows, each around the 800g mark, and to smoke them over hickory.

The secret is to ensure the fish are very fresh. I usually visit a trout farm in Victoria's Yarra Valley for these, catch them for myself, whereupon the farm will clean them for you and put them immediately into an ice slurry.

At home, I immerse them in a gentle brine of ½ cup of sea salt and ½ cup of brown sugar dissolved in 1 litre of water. Add a few lemon slices and a few slices of fresh ginger to the brine, and cure the trout in it for at least two hours, but not longer than four.

Fire up a suitable smoker – I find the Weber Smoker Mountain to be ideal for this job – and add a few wet hickory chunks and a couple of handfuls of hickory chips. Place the fish, on an oiled trivet if you like, on the top grill and cover for 90 minutes to two hours.

Remove the fish, still on the trivet. Let them cool and set, then refrigerate them overnight. To serve, peel the skin back carefully and accompany the delicate, smoked flesh with a sauce of grated, fresh horseradish folded through crème fraîche or sour cream, to taste.

Smoked trout can be served with a mound of potato salad, and is especially good on sandwiches or in salads, or flaked and used in pasta dishes. But be warned. Once you have smoked and eaten your own trout, you are unlikely to be satisfied with the store-bought version, ever again.

And if you happen to be a fly-fisherman, be further warned: your environmental resolve in terms of returning all fish caught to the stream, whether you need to or not, will be sorely tested once you have eaten your own home-smoked trout.

NOTE: To avoid the skin of the trout tearing when you remove them from the grill, it is necessary to hang the fish, from a string run through the eye cavities, in the smoke. This can be done with small fish, but is a bit of a fiddle. And what's a bit of torn skin between friends?

SALMON BURGERS: from glorious leftovers

And now for those off-cuts: I suggest you turn them, immediately, into salmon burgers which will set to perfection in your fridge and be fine to oil up and throw on the barbecue up to a day after you have made them.

700G OF SALMON OFFCUTS

½ RED ONION

2 TBS DIJON MUSTARD

1 TBS CHOPPED CAPERS

PANKO BREADCRUMBS

CIABATTA ROLLS

FRESH DILL

MAYONNAISE

SOUR CREAM

KOSHER DILL PICKLES

LEMON

Try this:

Collect about 700g of the salmon off-cuts, remembering the fatty cubes of belly salmon cut from the centre fillets you trimmed to cook on a plank. Drop half a red onion into a food processor and pulse a couple of times to chop. Add the salmon with 2 tsp of Dijon mustard and pulse a couple more times to chop the salmon coarsely and combine with the onion and mustard.

Tip into a bowl and fold through 1 tbs chopped capers and a handful of panko (Japanese) breadcrumbs to dry the mixture. Mix well, shape into four burgers, then cover with plastic wrap and refrigerate. They will be ready to cook in an hour, but will keep overnight.

To prepare the salmon burgers, split two ciabatta rolls; make a dill mayo by stirring finely chopped fresh dill through Best Foods bottled mayo with a dollop of sour cream.

Fire up a barbecue – gas or charcoal both work well – for direct grilling. Oil each of the salmon patties and cook for a total of about four minutes on the first side, turning through 90 degrees after two minutes. Flip and cook for four more minutes, turning through 90 degrees after two.

Rest, loosely tented with foil, as you lightly grill the buns. Spread the cut sides with dill mayo, place a salmon patty on each base, top with a few thin slices of large, kosher-style dill pickles and a squeeze of lemon. Put the top on your burger. Eat. And never again say an unkind word, or even have an unkind thought, about aquaculture.

TUNA: the other steak

These are hard words for any devout carnivore to swallow, but here they are: there are other, non-meat dishes with as much to contribute to the well-being of the human race as the perfect steak. There, I've said it.

TUNA STEAKS (SLABS)
EV OLIVE OIL
GRILLED TURNIP SLICES
SALT
CRACKED PEPPER

ANCHOVY MAYO:
ANCHOVY FILLETS
MAYONNAISE
SOUR CREAM

And of those dishes, my absolute favourite is an exquisitely grilled slab of tuna: seared, perfectly grill-marked, and cooked to the point where the interior is gloriously rare.

Buy the most generous slab you can imagine eating of the best, freshest, sashimi-grade tuna money can buy. Or rather, buy one of these per person. Starting with yourself, naturally.

The size and thickness of your steak, neatly trimmed of skin and bloodline, perhaps by your diligent fishmonger, will determine the cooking time. For a slab at least 3cm thick, try my timing. And if you are not happy with it, make a note to adjust next time.

Ensure, as always, your grill is clean, hot and freshly oiled. Smoke, for once, will have little impact. But over charcoal, toss on a handful of wet hickory chips anyway.

Oil (in EV olive oil) and season the tuna simply with sea salt and freshly ground black pepper. Place on the grill at 45 degrees to the grill bars, cover with the hood, and leave for just 45 seconds. Lift the lid and turn the tuna through 90 degrees, and cover for 30 seconds. Lift the lid and flip over. Cook for 30 seconds, covered, turn through 90 degrees and cook for 30 seconds, covered. Lift off the grill on to a warm plate to rest.

This should deliver a beautifully seared piece of fish that is still deliciously rare in the middle. Adjust to your own taste by all means, but never cook tuna all the way through because it will quickly become dry and indigestible and, frankly, you will have committed a sin so unpardonable you may never recover from it.

To serve the fish, plate it alongside a few discs of oiled, seasoned and seared turnip slices, or a similar grilled veg, and a dollop of anchovy mayo – made by chopping anchovy fillets and stirring them into Best Foods mayo and sour cream. I use a small tin of anchovy fillets with about 4 tbs of mayo and 2 tbs of sour cream.

To find a more delicious grilled steak dish than this you will have to search long and hard ... possibly in this book's meat section.

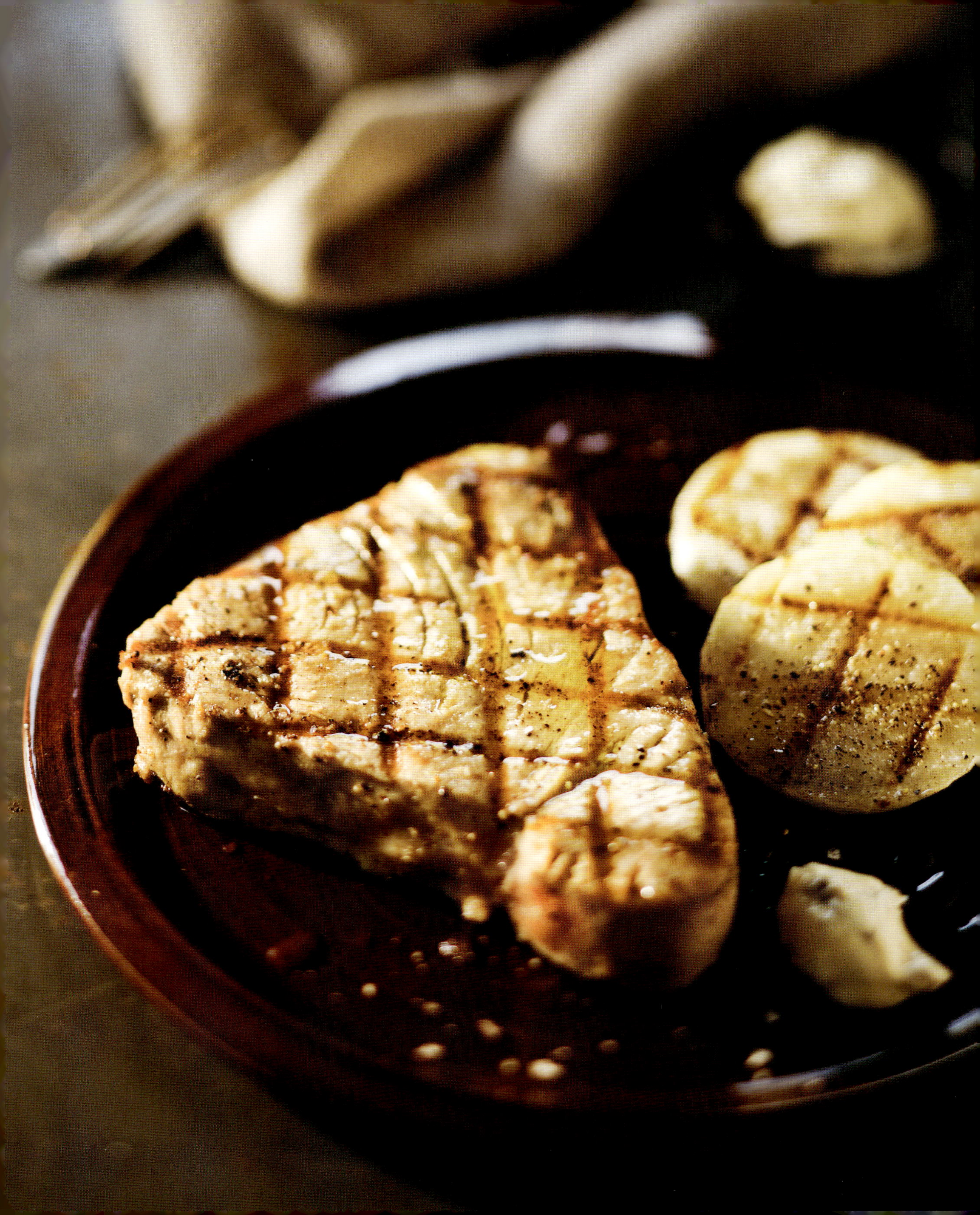

MEAT

MIGHTY MEAT: king of the barbecue jungle

For most barbecuists – even serious ones – meat is what sweating over a hot grill is all about. But for too many, sadly, the barbecue process leads to the serious abuse of blameless meat, rather than the enlightened enhancement of it.

As a nation, Australians – especially male family members who feel responsible for barbecue duties, despite the fact that, for many of them, the kitchen is a foreign land – are enthusiastic consumers but shamelessly poor cookers of meat.

In this section, I will attempt to redress a few of the issues that bring this about. But to kick things off, let me say just one thing: pink may not be every man's favourite colour. But when it comes to premium cuts of meat on the grill, it should become your colour of choice.

Cook a premium cut of anything to a basic grey, or even a nasty brown, and it will be, essentially, tough, inedible and indigestible. And it will mean the animal whose life was sacrificed to provide you with that fine cut died in vain.

And yes, lesser cuts are exceptions: ribs are cooked and smoked long and slowly. A brisket or a pork shoulder spend lifetimes in the swirling smoke and gentle heat. But for the rest, remember: pink, when it comes to red meat, is a manly colour, OK?

But let's start at the beginning ... with beef.

Because beef, surely, is the noblest of meats – especially when it is of premium quality, dry-aged and, where appropriate, exquisitely marbled. I am tempted to add the words "grass-fed", but that is a personal preference: I prefer grass-fed, but I have to confess to having eaten some grain-fed or grain-finished beef almost as good as any grass-fed beef I have tasted.

Beef, in all of its majesty, offers the full range of barbecue opportunities and challenges: some regard it as the easiest meat to barbecue, while others seem able to demonstrate, effortlessly, that it is possibly the hardest.

I find it difficult to decide which, in fact, is the greater barbecue crime: overcooking a prime cut of beef, such as a rib-eye steak on the bone, or undercooking a secondary cut, like a brisket. Either offence, in my view, should carry, for the perpetrator, a mandatory six-month suspension of grilling rights, with the first month on an enforced vegan diet. No exceptions. And none of that suspended sentence nonsense.

THE SERIOUS RIBS: making a stand

Among primary cuts of beef, the noblest of all, surely, is the cut that I call a standing rib – also known as a baron of beef, just to confirm the nobility I mentioned earlier. It is a glorious portion of the beast which, at its best, offers well-marbled meat under a generous layer of fat that works its magic during the cooking. It is a fine cut for oven-roasting, but even better cooked over indirect heat in a charcoal barbecue, swathed in hickory smoke.

A BARON OF BEEF
EV OLIVE OIL
SEA SALT
FRESH ROSEMARY
BLACK PEPPER
FRESH HORSERADISH
CRÉME FRAÎCHE

The cut – and if serious indulgence is your thing, request your ribs cut from the end with the fillet attached, making it the biggest, fattest T-bone you have ever seen – needs little more than a quick massage with EV olive oil and a generous sprinkle of sea salt, freshly ground black pepper and chopped, fresh rosemary.

From there, it is simply a matter of controlling the temperature, ensuring the meat does not overcook and resting it adequately.

For medium-rare, which is the most you should ever cook this cut, remove the meat from the heat when the internal temperature reaches 40-45°C, and rest it for at least 20 minutes, loosely tented in foil.

Mustards and horseradish sauces are all very well, but the best condiment for roast beef is freshly made horseradish cream – a fresh horseradish root, peeled and grated into crème fraîche with a pinch of salt.

Nothing more.

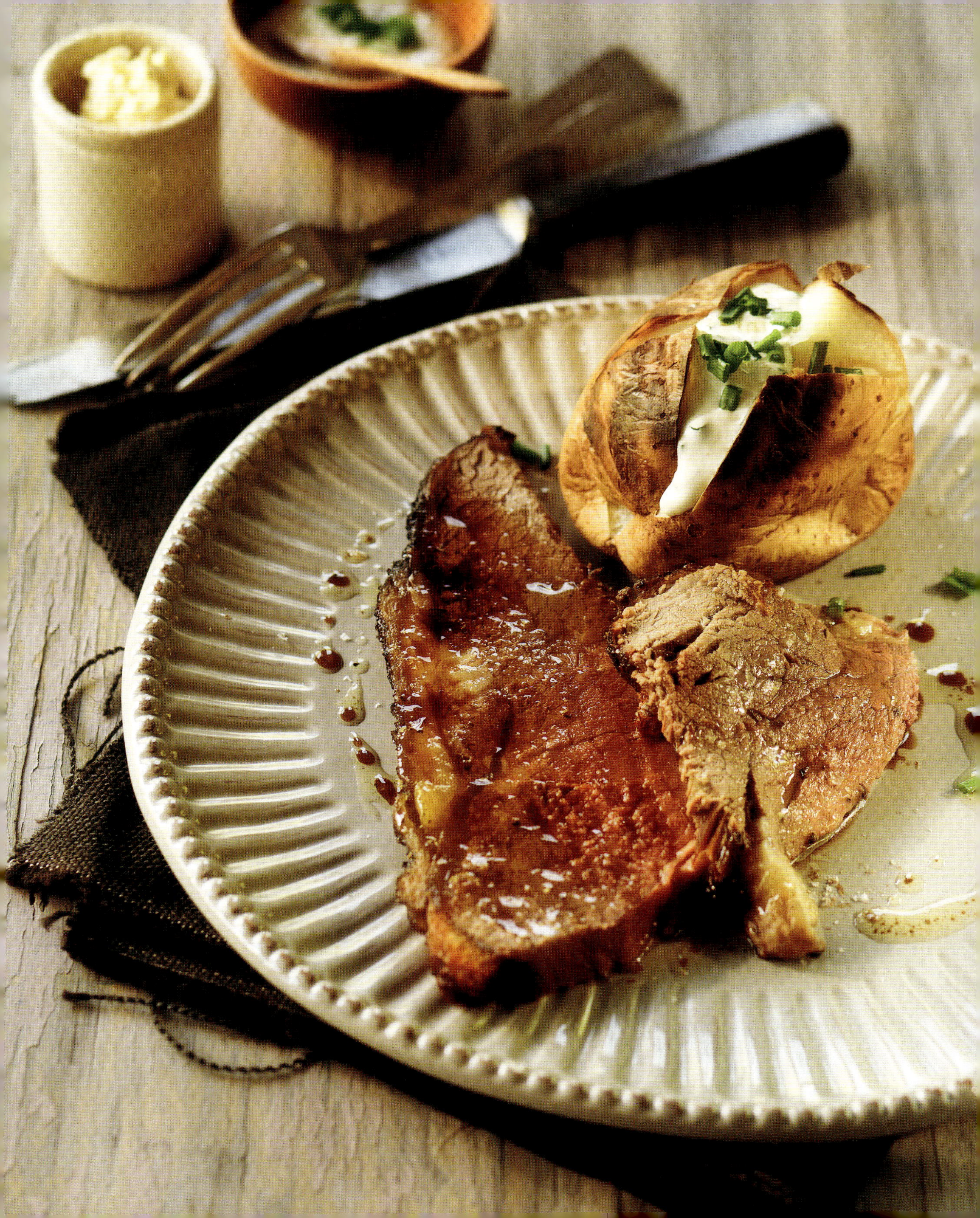

BRISKET: smoking it slowly

Ask a Texan dude about barbecue, and he will start talking about brisket. In fact, ask a Texan about anything, and he will probably start talking about brisket.

BRISKET

ALL-PURPOSE RUB

MOP SAUCE

APPLE JUICE

BARBECUE OR HORSERADISH SAUCE

COLESLAW

BREAD ROLLS

And if you want to eat the best brisket on the planet, head for Texas. Or, if that is not convenient just at the moment, ask your butcher to provide you with a fine, fat-topped brisket and try this:

Rub the beef – which could easily weigh 3-4kg if it is the entire cut, which I prefer – with my all-purpose rub (page 11) and rest it, at room temperature, for at least an hour.

Fire up your smoker – I use either an off-set barrel smoker or a Weber Smokey Mountain for this job – and, when the temperature is in the smoke zone, or around the 110°C mark, toss wet chunks and chips of a suitable wood such as hickory or mesquite on the charcoal and place the beef on the (lower in the Weber SM) rack.

The first cooking stage, during which you should moisten the meat with a mop sauce (page 12) every hour, will take about six hours, or until the internal temperature of the meat reaches 70°C.

At this point, lift the meat off the grill and double-wrap it in foil, pouring a cup of apple juice into the foil to moisten the meat further. Seal the foil and return the meat to the smoker for another two hours, or until the internal temperature reaches 85°C.

Remove from the grill, rest, slice and serve the tender, richly flavoured meat on rolls with barbecue sauce and coleslaw and perhaps a side of beans or, for something a bit more refined, use the fresh horseradish sauce I described in the standing rib roast section, rather than a barbecue sauce.

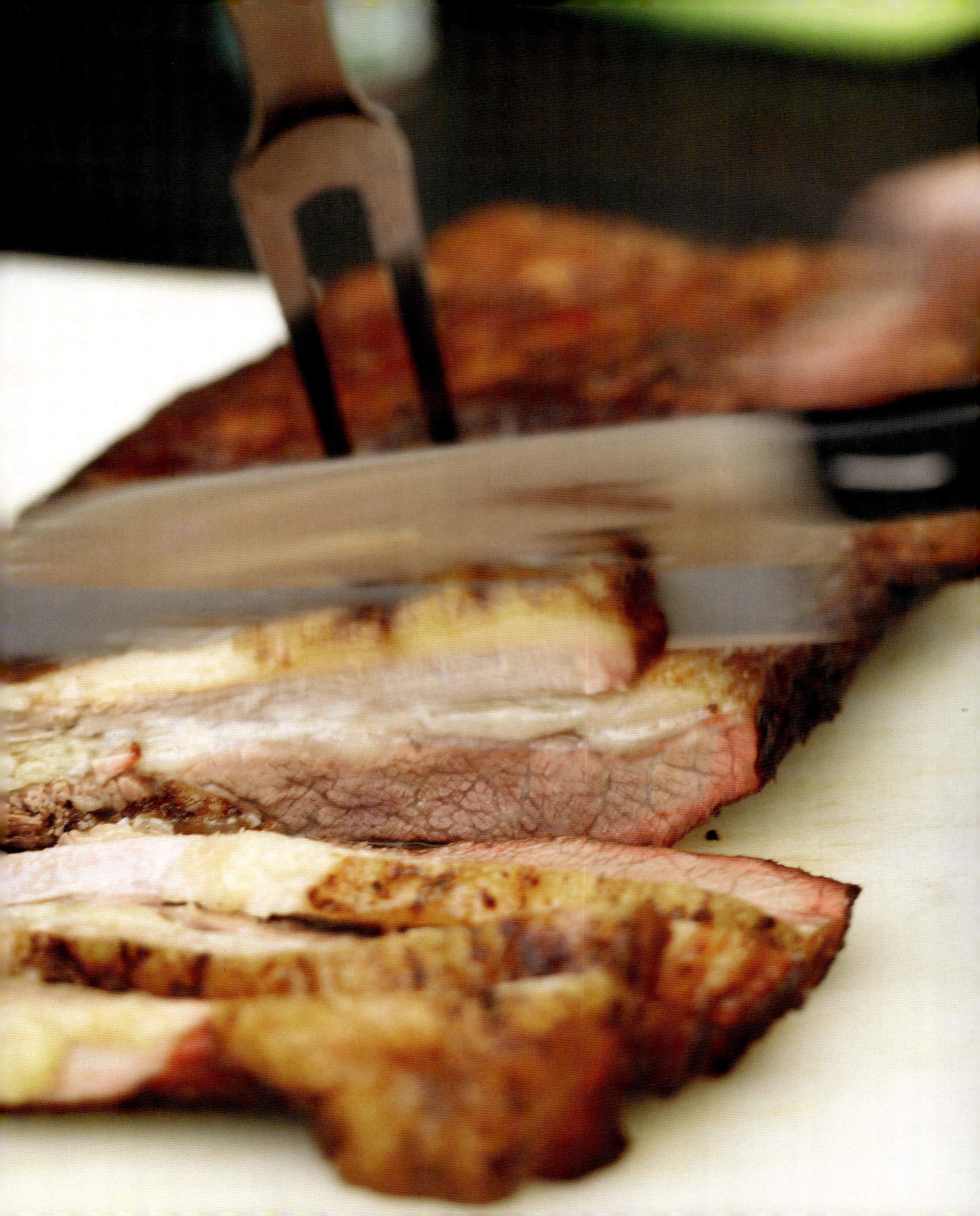

THE OTHER RIBS: it's not just a pork thing

They are not a million miles away from brisket, either geographically or in flavour and texture, but are cooked more like pork spare ribs.

BEEF RIBS

ALL-PURPOSE RUB

ALL-PURPOSE BARBECUE SAUCE

FRESH HORSERADISH

CRÉME FRAÎCHE

I refer, of course, to beef ribs – not necessarily short ribs, which are not a cheap cut, but the rest of the rib knocked into three sections, each around 8-10cm.

To extract the ultimate result from these, treat them exactly like pork spare ribs (page 74). But remember how much more meat you are dealing with. So coat them generously with my all-purpose rub (page 11) and place in a resealable plastic bag in the fridge at least overnight, but two nights won't hurt.

Now, fire up the Weber Smokey Mountain with plenty of hickory chunks and chips and place the ribs on the grill over a full water-bath. Rather than just the couple of hours pork ribs will require, give these babies four of the best at a smoking temperature not too far above 100ºC, topping up the hickory just once, after the first hour or so.

Then, take them off, and apply the "Texas Crutch" – an ingenious technique, allegedly of Texan origin, for enhancing the moistness and tenderness of barbecued meat. Brush them generously with my all-purpose barbecue sauce, wrap them well in foil and return to the smoker to braise for at least another 3 hours. At which point, take them off, open the foil, and prepare to be truly astonished by how good they are.

You may find it a step too far, but a little of that fresh horseradish in crème fraîche we used with the standing rib and possibly the brisket works wonders with these, also.

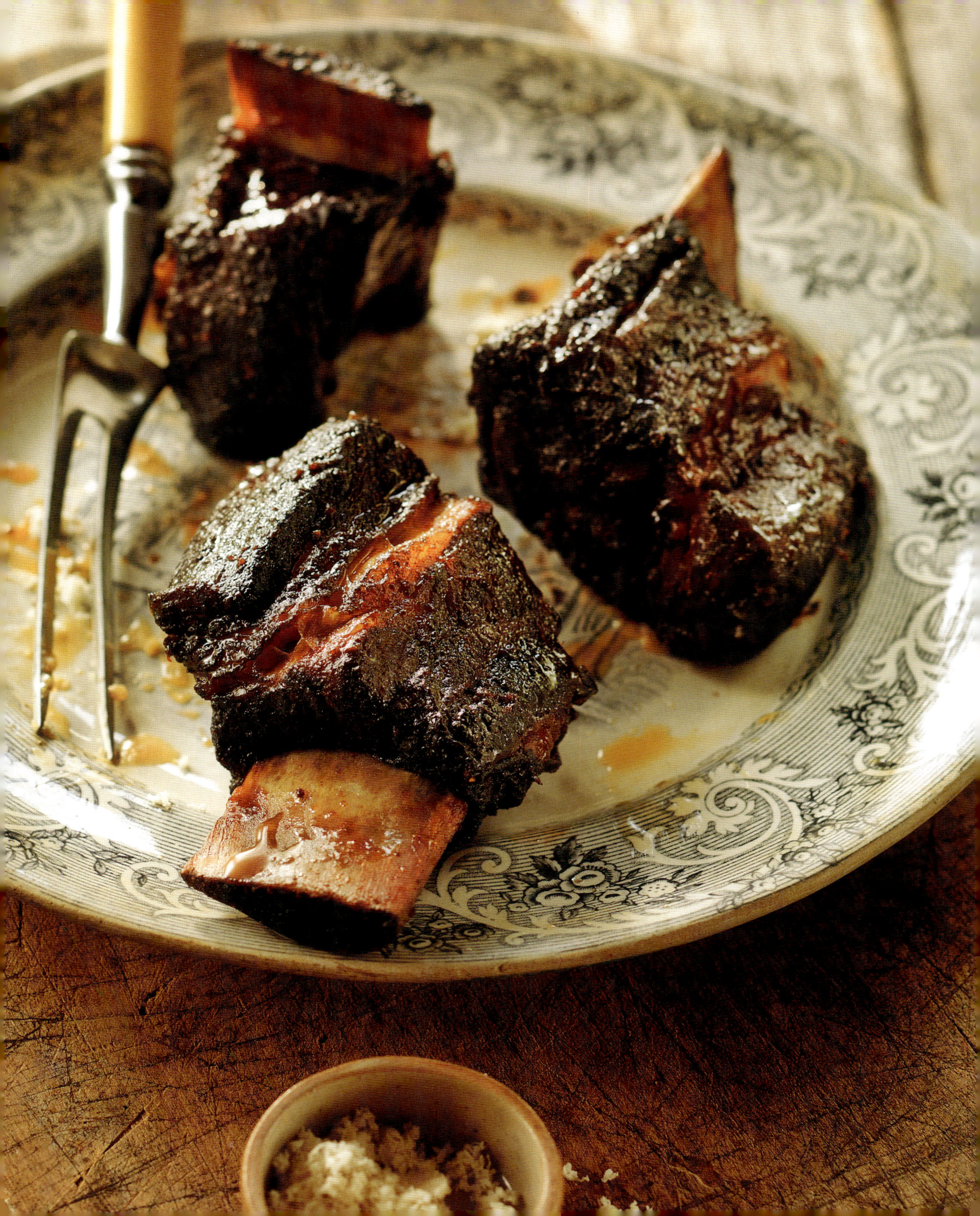

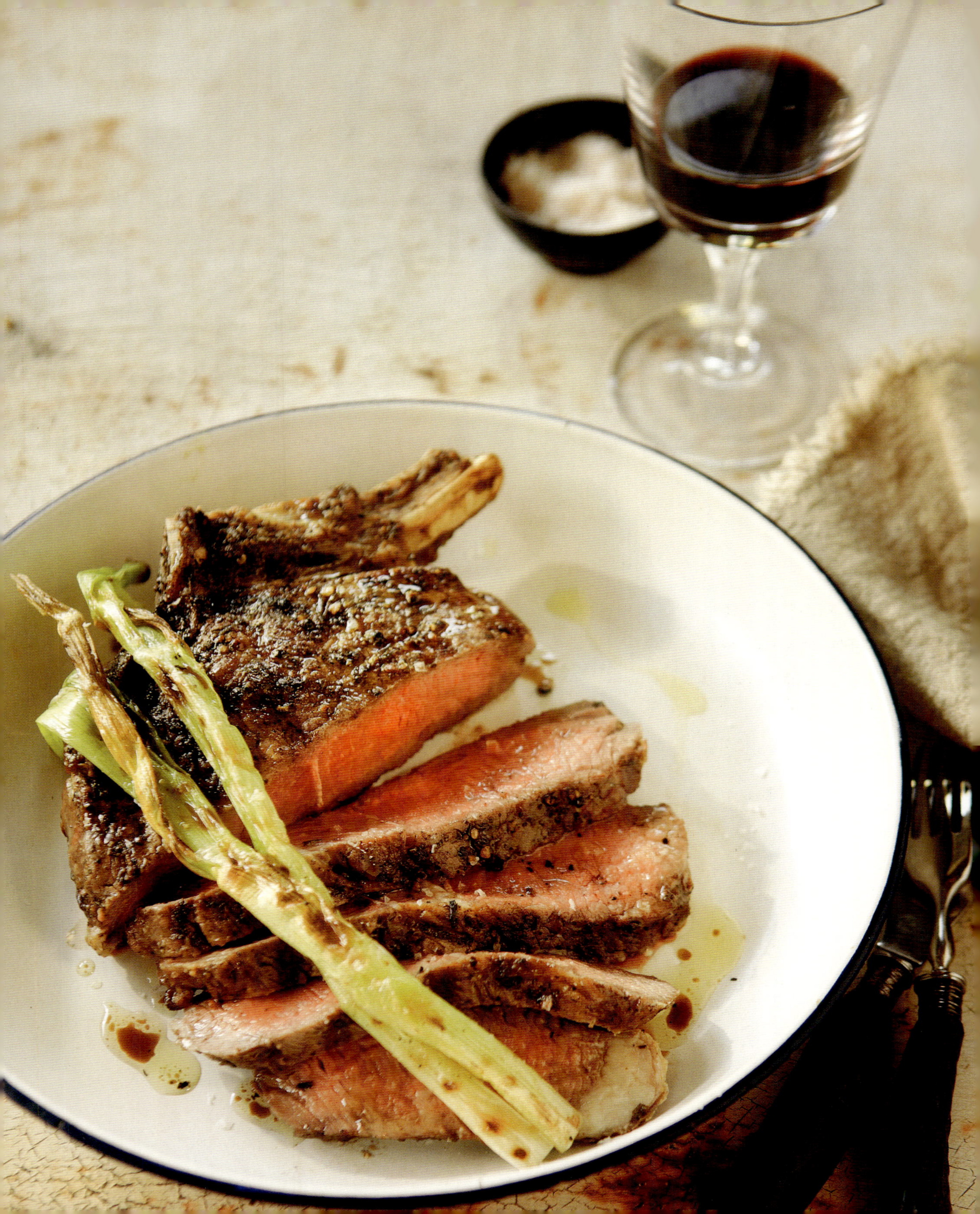

STEAK: striving for perfection

It sounds too good to be true, and you've probably heard it all before. But for many devout grillmasters, this is the Holy Grail – a steak so good that it will take your breath away. And while I recognise the dangers in making outrageous claims, let me simply say that I have arrived at a cooking method for a rib eye steak on the bone which I will regard as perfect, at least until something better comes along.

2 MONSTROUS RIB EYES

SWEET POTATOES

SPRING ONIONS

UNSALTED BUTTER

BUTTERMILK

MAPLE SYRUP

FOR THE SPECIAL RUB:

50G SMOKED SEA SALT

2 TBS FRESH BLACK PEPPERCORNS

1 TBS CHILLI FLAKES

1 TBS FRESH ROSEMARY NEEDLES

This is a recipe for just two steaks, but unless you are dealing with very serious eaters indeed, they will feed four people.

Try this:

Buy two of those monstrous rib eyes on the bone that premium butchers sell these days – often vacuum-sealed. You are looking for examples weighing close to 600g each. If you settle for slightly smaller steaks, the method still works, but remember to scale back the cooking time. If you buy vacuum-sealed meat, take it out of the package at least four hours, or longer, before you cook it. Rinse and dry it, and place it on a metal rack over a shallow dish in the refrigerator until about two hours before you plan to grill it. If your butcher has cut you fresh steaks – ideally from a dark, dry-aged *cote de boeuf* – still rest them, uncovered, on a rack in the fridge until two hours before grill time.

Now, make a special rub for this dish. It is a fairly ferocious one, and I would not ever suggest using it on a single, one-person steak, such as a porterhouse. But it is perfect for this recipe for which you slice the steak before serving, which means each slice has simply a crusting of the rub, rather than a complete coating. So, using a mortar and pestle, pound together 50g of a smoked sea salt (Maldon make an excellent one, or use plain sea salt if you can't find smoked), 2 tbs fresh black peppercorns, 1 tbs chilli flakes and 1 tbs of freshly picked rosemary needles, removed from the stems. Pound this mixture thoroughly, grinding against the sides of the mortar, to create a well-blended rub.

Fire up a powerful gas barbecue or a charcoal barbecue such as a Weber kettle or a Big Green Egg for direct cooking. Grill bars are essential – hot plates, as all budding grillmasters should know by now, must never be used for cooking steak. Or indeed, anything else. If there is something you feel you need to cook on a hot plate (an egg, for example), then cook it in a pan, not on a barbecue. But, back to our steak: the inside temperature of, say, a three-burner barbecue such as a Weber Genesis will soon hit the 250ºC mark. Lower all the levels to about three quarters. Ensure your grill is clean and oiled, as well as being very, very hot.

Now, drizzle your two steaks with EV olive oil to coat all sides and sprinkle all over with the rub. Place the steaks on the grill at an angle of 45 degrees to the grill bars and drop the hood.

After 3 minutes, lift the lid and turn the steaks through 90 degrees and, again, drop the hood. After 3 more minutes, flip the steaks over and repeat the process on the second side. Then, lift the steaks from the grill, place them on a rack over a baking dish and loosely tent with foil for at least 10 minutes.

The steaks should now be cooked to perfection – on the rare side of medium rare. If you must have them cooked more than that, add a minute to each position. Finish them with a squeeze of lemon and slice them, thickly, from the outside of the meat, in towards, and parallel to, the bone. Divide the meat between four plates – I like to serve them with mashed sweet potato (finished with unsalted butter, a dollop of buttermilk and a splash of maple syrup) and a couple of oiled, seasoned and quickly grilled spring onions with each serving. But I suspect the flavour of the meat will amaze you, whatever you choose to serve it with.

The object, here, is to use a bold, spicy rub which the meat, because it is thick, can handle. Also, by cooking it quickly at high heat, you are deeply caramelising – almost charring – the outsides of the steaks. This charred flavour, enhanced by flames that may well rise, briefly, inside your barbecue, will contrast exquisitely with the moist, pink centre of the thick steaks. Thinner steaks would be destroyed by this approach.

There is room, obviously, for you to adjust this approach to your own taste. If, for example, your steaks weigh 500g each, cook them less in each position. And remember: you will have paid plenty for these steaks, so for heaven's sake, don't bloody overcook them!

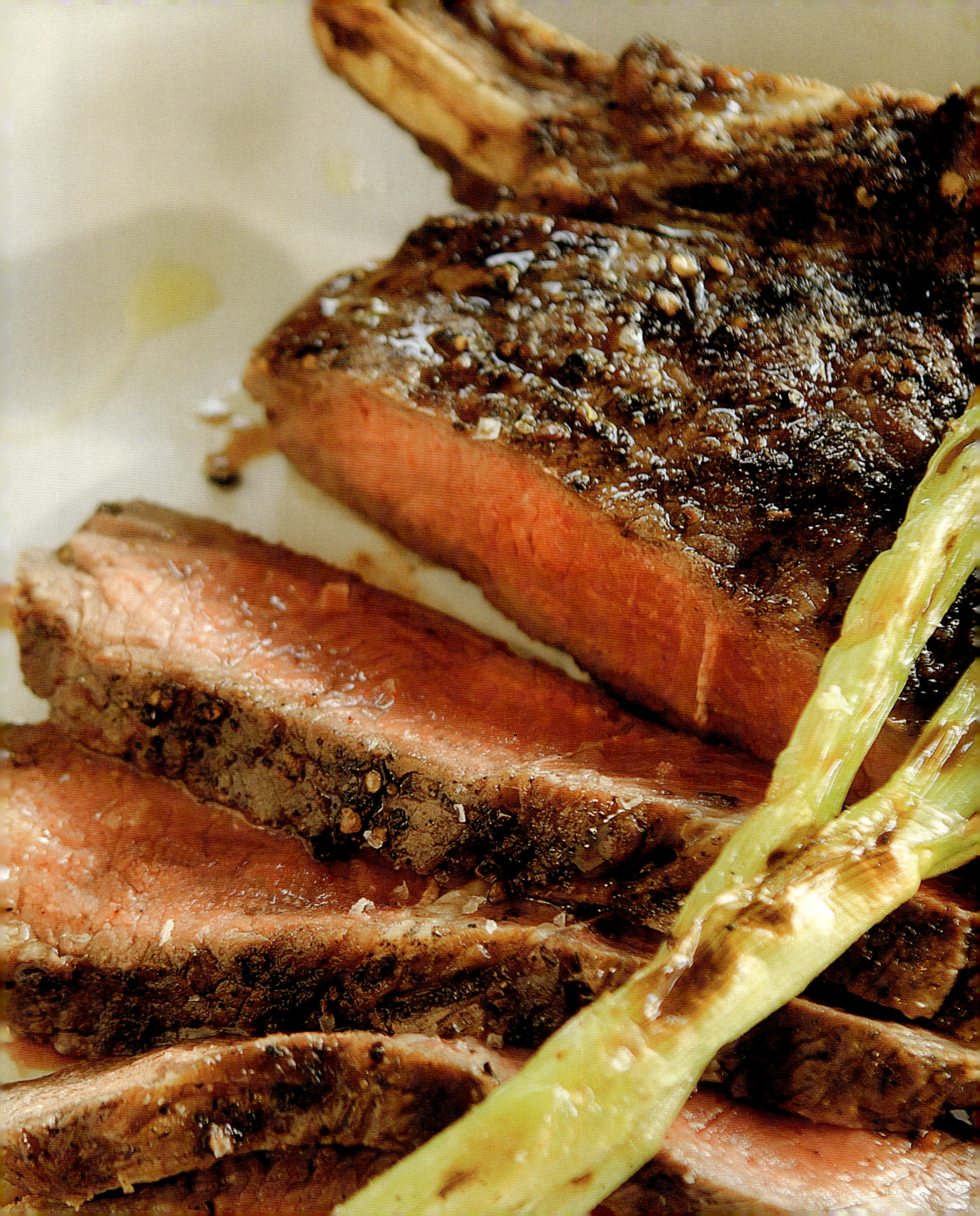

ENTRECÔTE: it's French for a terrific steak

The French, and the English for that matter, call our porterhouse steak an entrecôte, while Americans call it a New York sirloin. It's the same, cracking piece of meat by any name, however. But it is the French, clearly, who have developed perhaps the most interesting way of barbecuing it.

PORTERHOUSE STEAK
BEEF BONE MARROWS
SHALLOTS
EV OLIVE OIL
RED WINE SAUCE
VINE CLIPPINGS (TO TOSS ON THE FIRE)

There, especially in the glorious wine region of Bordeaux, you will encounter a dish called entrecôte bordelaise. It's a cracker. To make it for yourself you will need a couple of extra items...

First of all, to garnish the steak, you will need some chopped bone marrow – any butcher worth his salt will split a couple of beef bone marrows for you to scrape out – and a small, square, cast iron pan. You will also need a quantity of dry vine clippings, which you can usually get from your nearest vineyard. These are essential, also. Place them in a bowl of water.

Fire up a charcoal grill for direct cooking – a Weber kettle or a Big Green Egg are ideal – to a blistering heat. Place the cast iron pan on the grill and cover the barbecue. When the pan is very hot, toss a few handfuls of the soaked vine clippings on the fire, oil and season a thick entrecôte and place on the clean, oiled grill, at 45 degrees to the grill bars. After about a minute and a half – or more or less, according to the thickness of the steak – turn through 90 degrees and cover the barbecue for a similar length of time.

Now, flip the steak, top the cooked side with a good layer of chopped beef bone marrow and chopped shallots which you have tossed together with a little EV olive oil and seasoned well, and place the hot, cast-iron pan on top of the steak, covering the bone marrow and shallots. Using gloves or a mitt, obviously. At the half-way mark, again, carefully turn the steak through 90 degrees, leaving the pan in place. And at either the two or three minute mark, depending on the thickness of your steak, it will be cooked. And magnificent.

A simple red wine sauce will complete the picture if you are feeling in an expansive mood. And a glass of your finest cabernet sauvignon or merlot – the grapes of Bordeaux – will also help.

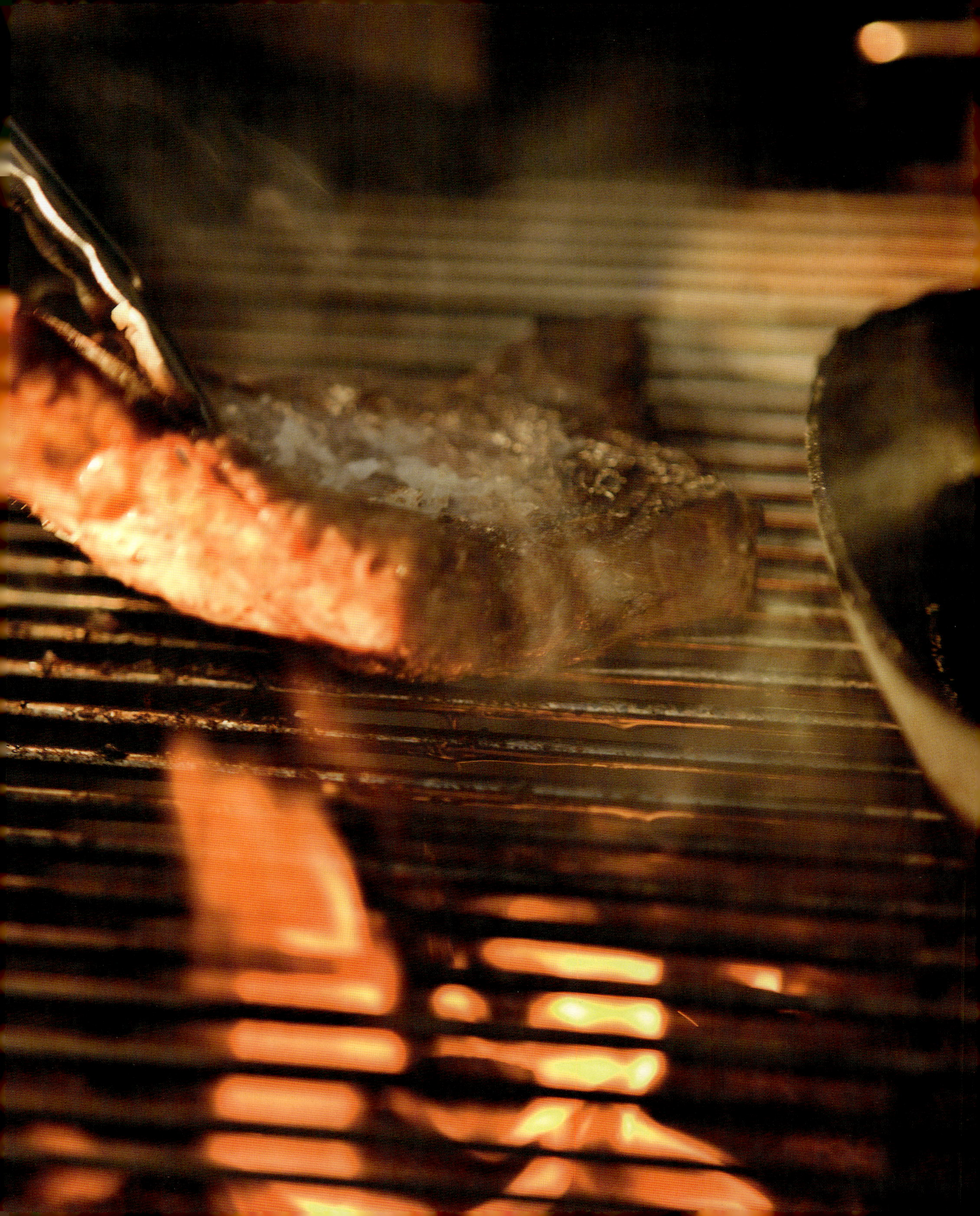

PORK: a meat born to barbecue

In barbecue terms, there is no unsuitable cut of pork. It's just that some cuts of pork, luxuriating over flames and enveloped in clouds of hickory smoke, are even more suitable than others, as George Orwell, equally, might have noted.

The roasting joints, skin on of course, are magnificent. Prove this to yourself by cooking a loin – bone in, ideally, or boned and rolled if you insist – indirectly, either on a gas barbecue with the centre element turned off, in a Weber Q on a trivet over a rectangle of double foil or, best of all, in a Weber kettle with both charcoal baskets full, and plenty of wet hickory sending up lots of aromatic, pork-friendly smoke.

Carefully score the meat of your joint (a leg responds well to similar treatment but involves a longer roasting time, obviously) evenly and carefully: a Stanley knife makes the best job of this.

Then, rub sea-salt into each score and finally drizzle some olive oil over the pork. Place it in the centre of the hot barbecue for 20 to 40 minutes at full heat, or until the skin blisters around the cuts. Then, either turn down the gas to low, or reduce the kettle heat by decreasing the airflow.

Leave it to cook through, or until your meat thermometer registers around 70°C. Rest it, loosely tented, for about 20 minutes and ... you may find yourself seriously considering the possibility of adopting a recently orphaned pig, as a way of showing your gratitude.

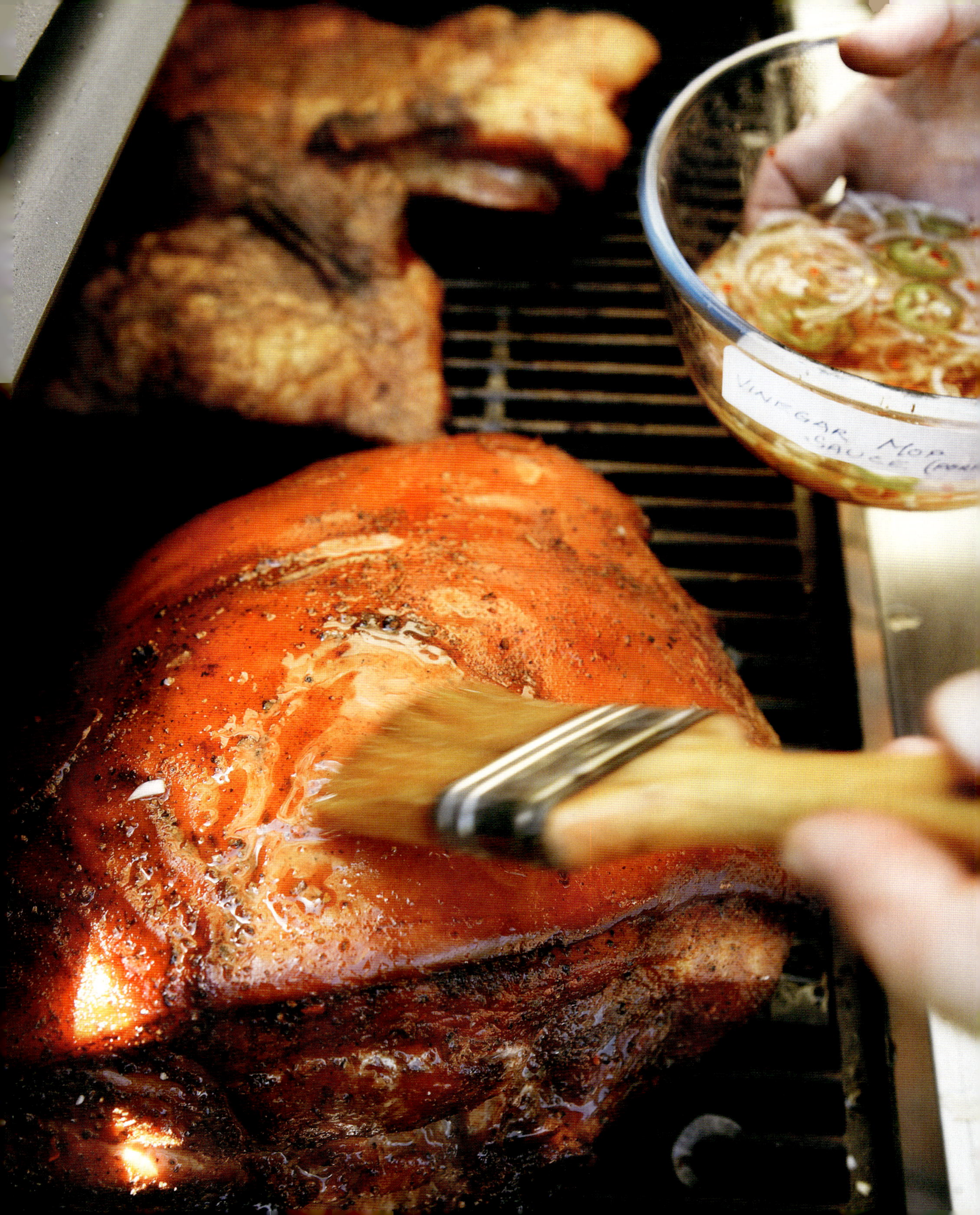
VINEGAR MOP
SAUCE

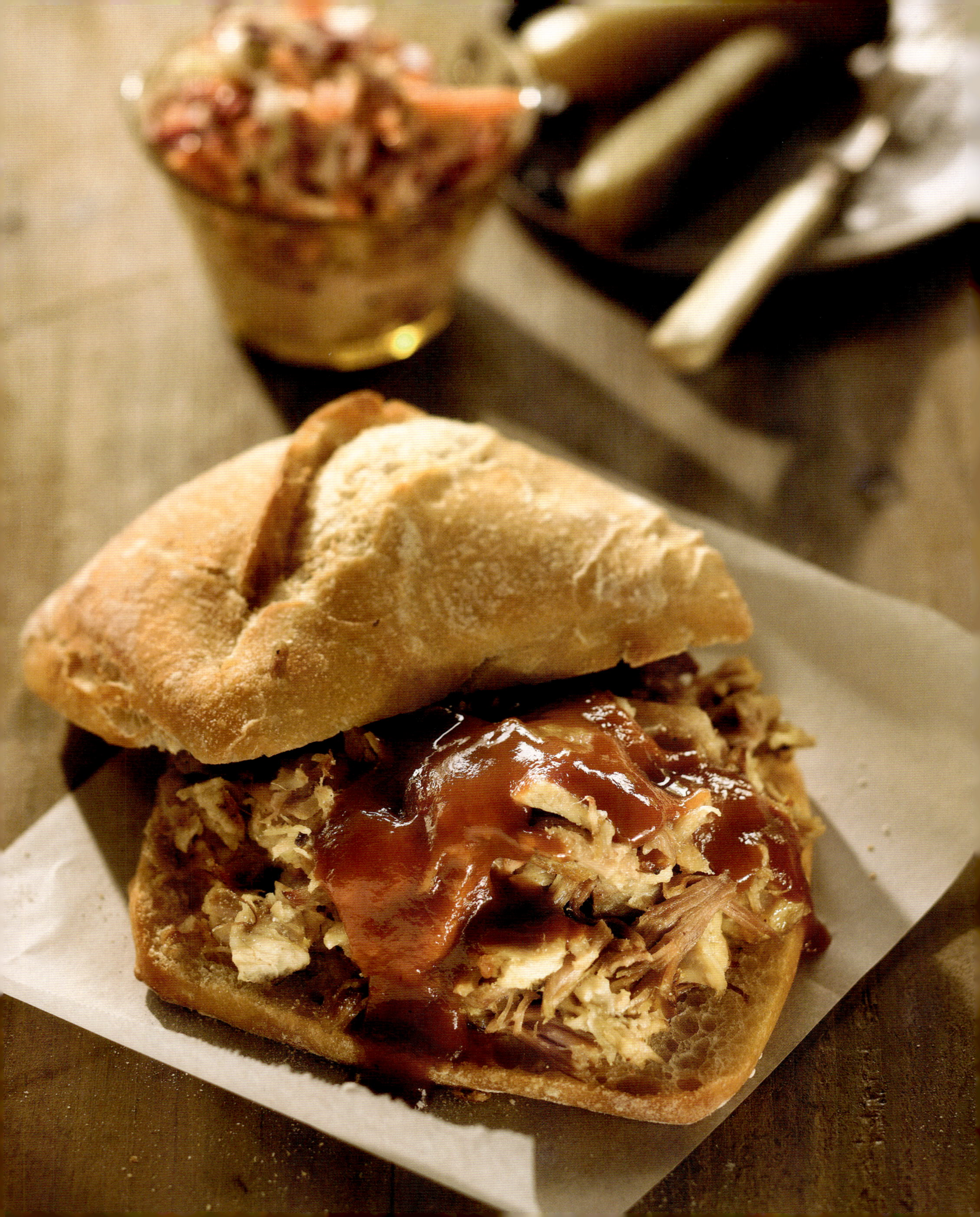

PULLED PORK: the stuff of legends

When you mention barbecue in most states of the union, it does not mean quite what it means in Australia. Rather, it means this dish – slowly, smokily cooked pork shoulder, pulled apart or chopped (depending on your religion, the set of your jib, or some such thing), sauced and crammed into a roll with coleslaw. And suddenly, it all makes sense. Try it for yourself:

PORK SHOULDER
ALL-PURPOSE RUB
MOP SAUCE
BARBECUE SAUCE
COLESLAW
BARBECUE BUNS

Massage plenty of my all-purpose rub (page 11) into a skinless or skin-on slab of pork shoulder – you can decide on skin status: there are strengths in both methods.

Let it rest at room temperature for at least an hour while you prepare your smoker, as for ribs. Place the pork on the rack and, every hour or so, mop it with mop sauce (page 17).

It will take at least six hours to cook, and quite possibly a lot longer than that, to the point where it is gloriously tender, and the meat thermometer registers an internal temperature of almost 90°C.

Rest it, loosely tented, for 20 minutes or so while you warm the rolls and tune up your coleslaw. Discard the skin if you had left it on (which I do, incidentally) and pull the pork apart, or chop it (my preference – and you can chop a little of the skin to go in with it, if you like), and serve generous portions of it, splashed with my all-purpose barbecue sauce, with plenty of coleslaw, on commercial barbecue buns.

It's all about observing the barbecue traditions, OK? Also, it's slightly magnificent served this way.

NOTE: Use of the Texas Crutch technique mentioned in the pork ribs recipe can also be used with a pork shoulder. I prefer this slightly more purist method, but if you have trouble getting the pork as moist and tender as you would like it, get out the foil and the barbecue sauce, and work that magic for a few more hours.

CUTLETS: the magic is in the brine

A pork cutlet is a distinguished cut of pig with sweet, delicate meat in the eye, and succulent meat with a good layer of delicious fat clinging to the bone.

4 PORK CUTLETS

EV OLIVE OIL

6 TBS OF APPLE, REDCURRANT OR QUINCE JELLY

1 TBS UNSALTED BUTTER

APPLE BRANDY

CIDER BRINE:

½ CUP OF SEA SALT

330ML CIDER

ROSEMARY

SAGE

THYME

BLACK PEPPER

Some butchers insist on "frenching" cutlets which, frankly, is an offence against nature. You pay more for less meat, so insist on the rib bone being left as is: unfrenched, and as nature intended.

Brining pork cutlets before exposing them to fierce heat, however, is a fine idea: it keeps them moist and helps maintain a springy texture. But, better still, cure them in a cider brine and you will lift their spirits significantly. And your own.

For four sturdy cutlets, on the bone and with or without skin, mix half a cup of sea salt with the contents of a 330ml bottle of cider. Add fresh herbs – I use a mixture of rosemary, sage and thyme – pounded in a mortar and pestle with black peppercorns.

Put the brine, with the cutlets, in a shallow dish or a large ziplock bag. Refrigerate for at least four hours, but never for longer than eight hours or they may become over-salted. Take them out of the fridge about half an hour before you cook them. Rinse and dry them, and then drizzle olive oil over them.

Your next responsibility is not to overcook them: in most parts of the world, that is no longer necessary. The faintest hint of pink in a cutlet or chop is not only acceptable, it is highly desirable.

Brush the cutlets after you lift them off the grill, or even just before, with a glaze made by warming 6 tbs of apple, redcurrant or quince jelly (not paste: clear jelly) with 1 tbs of unsalted butter until combined. Lift off and add a splash of apple brandy, ideally a rustic, local one. Serve extra glaze with the cutlets, if you like.

Start to cook them, as always, at 45 degrees to the grill bars. Turn them through 90 degrees after a quarter of the cooking time, turn them over after half the cooking time and repeat the 90-degree move on the second side. Cooking times depend on the thickness of the cutlets and the heat of your grill, but 2 minutes in each position, for a total of 8 minutes should be more than enough.

Glaze and rest the cutlets for 3-4 minutes, tented in foil, before eating. If, when you cut them, they are not moist and springy with just a hint of pink at the centre, then cook them less next time.

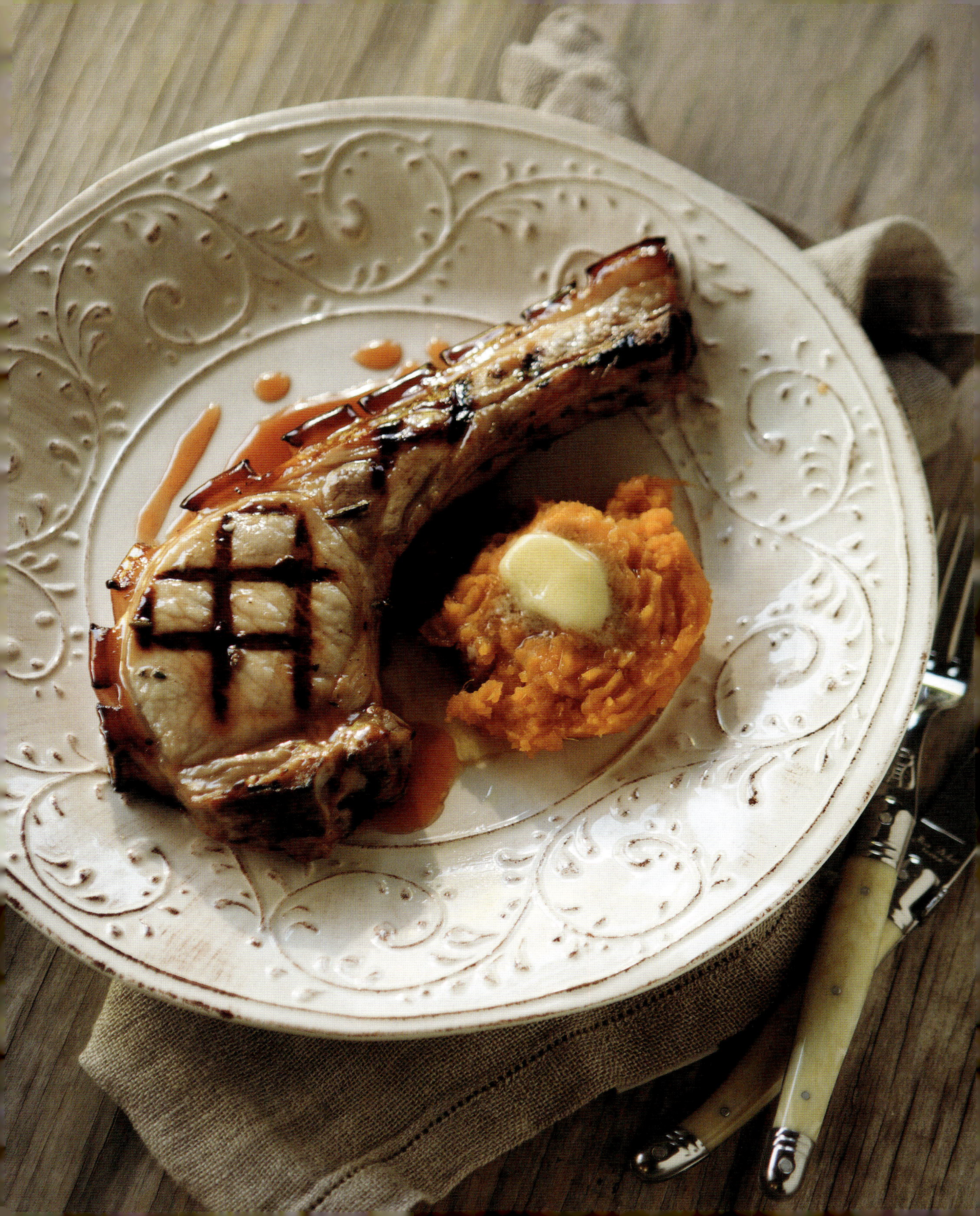

SPARE RIBS: making sense of smoke

If there is a single dish that defines American barbecue, this has to be it: racks of smoky, tender, succulent pork ribs with the strips of sweet meat barely clinging to the bone, the flavour dictated by the quality of the meat and the contents of your barbecue sauce.

PORK SPARE RIBS

ALL-PURPOSE RUB

ALL-PURPOSE BARBECUE SAUCE

The ribs are cured overnight in a rub, slowly smoked for a couple of hours over hickory chips and chunks – ideally in a Weber Smokey Mountain barbecue, off-set barrel smoker or similar – and then wrapped in foil and finished, in that familiar process known as the Texas Crutch, for at least another two hours, in that same hot and smoky environment.

But let's start from the beginning…

On the night before rib-day, remove the membrane from the back of two racks of American-style pork spare ribs (your butcher should know what you mean by this description of the ribs you need, but if he doesn't, get a new butcher) by lifting a corner of the membrane and grabbing hold with a piece of paper kitchen towel or, better still, a Chux. It will pull away, thus exposing the meat to the rub you are about to apply.

So now, apply my all-purpose rub, and place the ribs inside a very large zip-lock bag. Refrigerate overnight.

Set up the smoker for a long, slow, smoky cook by creating a base with a container of unlit briquettes or lump charcoal, and topping with a container of lit. Allow the fire to take hold, and then settle. Top the fire with wet hickory – some chunks for long smoking, and some chips to send up heavy smoke from the outset – before placing the ribs, in a rib rack, into the smoker.

The thermometer on the smoker should not be too far above 100°C at this point; half close the vents, or adjust as necessary, to achieve this. Smoke for 2-3 hours, or until you can see rib ends pulling away slightly from the meat.

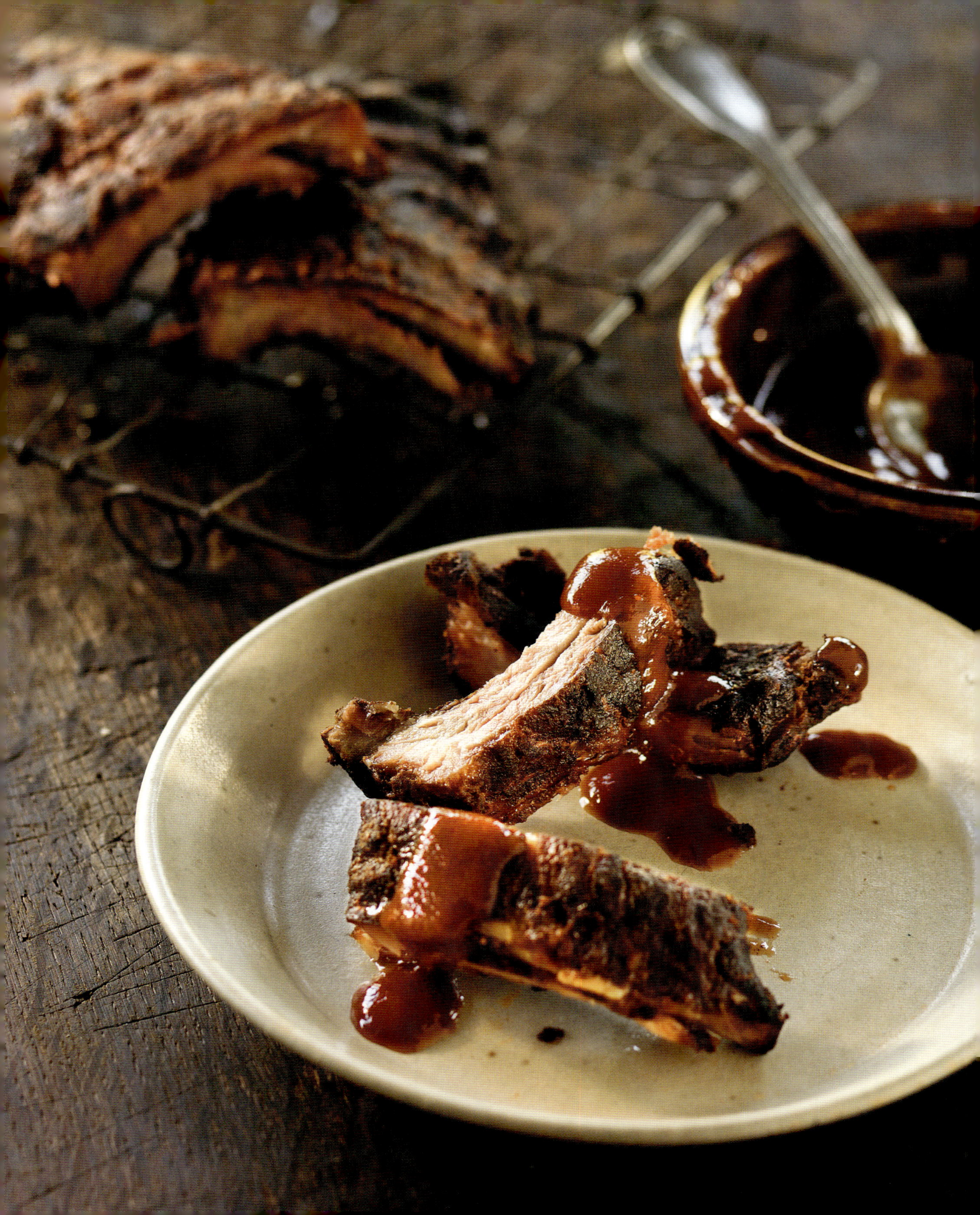

Remove the ribs from smoker, brush them generously with all-purpose barbecue sauce, double wrap the sauced racks in foil and return the closed foil package to the smoker to sit and re-moisturise in the gentle heat for at least two more hours.

For a Weber kettle, set up a two-level fire, let the coals burn well down before putting on the ribs, moderate the air flow to keep the heat low and smoke the ribs over the drip tray filled with water. Top it up as necessary.

When the racks have finally done their thing, take them off the smoker, unwrap them on a cutting board, slice them into individual ribs and serve with extra barbecue sauce on the side.

Eat one.

So now … do you understand what all the fuss is about?

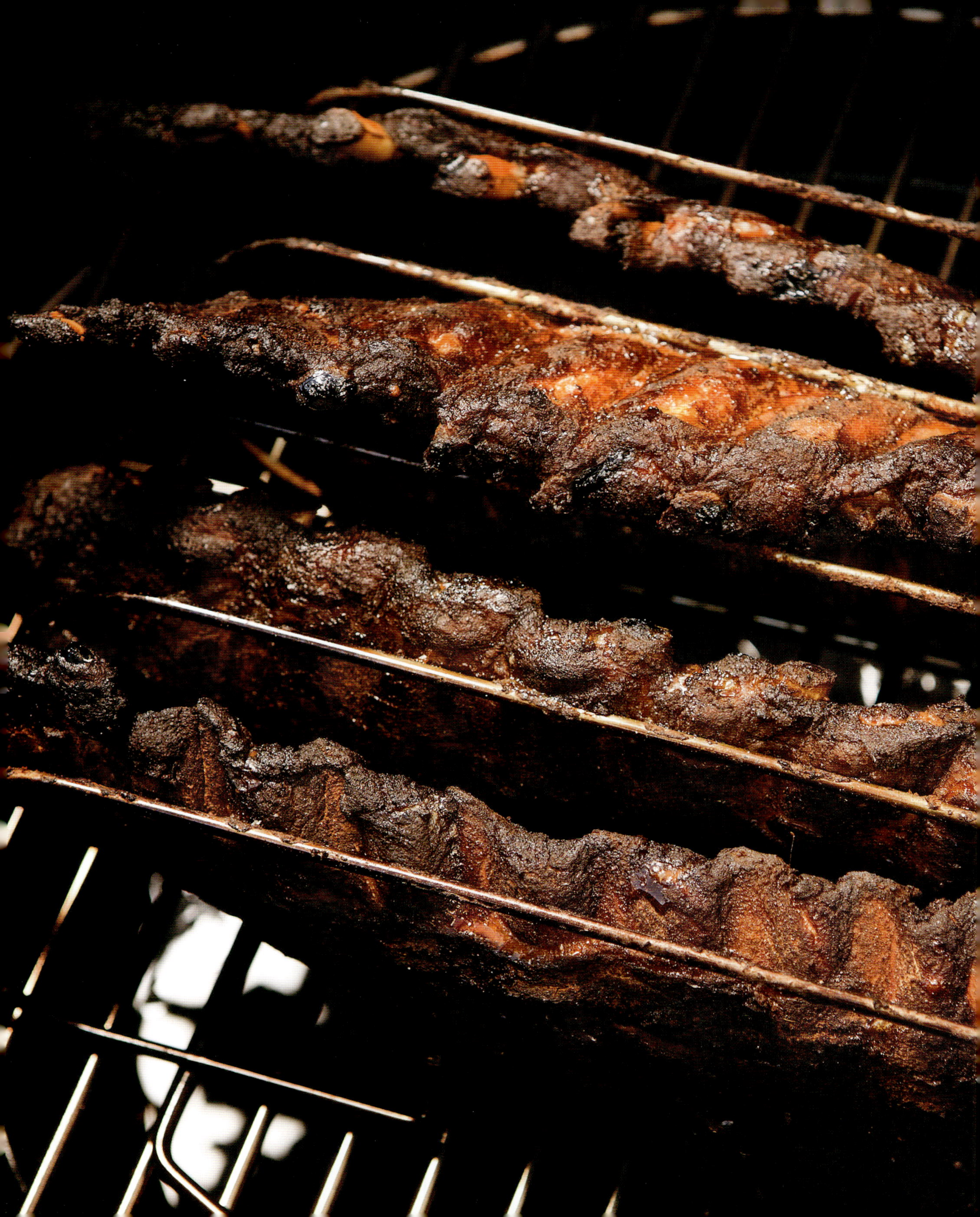

SAUSAGES: avoiding the snags

Snags, snorkers or mystery bags should be the simplest and most foolproof of barbecue offerings but, of course, they are not. Sausages – whether they are distinguished ones made from pure pork with perhaps a hint of fennel, or veal, sage and pine nut masterpieces, or fanciful (and undesirable, in my view) versions made from anything from chicken, cheese and vegemite to wombat droppings – are seriously abused in this country: we can, and should, do better.

Let's focus, then, on pure porkers – British cumberlands, perhaps, or French Toulouse or, my favourites, glorious Italian pure porkers skilfully created by Italian master butchers who understand the splendour of pig meat.

But first, hear this: if you are happy with the disgusting, charred apologies for snags served up at neighbourhood sausage sizzles or, worse still, adjacent to voting booths on election days, you have my sympathy. Also, for future reference, you are gastronomically challenged, and possibly deranged.

Because these – and I am focussing on the election day versions here – are probably responsible for the parlous state of our nation's political mediocrity. I am convinced those sausage sizzles are run by anarchists bent on creating political chaos, and succeeding. But I digress…

First, take your pure, perfect porkers. Then, blanch them, for a few minutes in a large pot of boiling water, allowing the water to return to a gentle simmer before you time the process. The idea here is not to have to worry about whether your snags are cooked through when they are on the grill, because you will know they are. And that is the time when perfectly good snags, as well are frightful ones, are reduced to burnt offerings, or worse.

After the blanching, drain the sausages and leave them to cool until you are ready to cook them. This, obviously, can be done well in advance. Now, lightly oil your cool snags and place them, at 45 degrees to the grill bars, as always, on a clean, hot, oiled grill. (Gas works well, but if you have a Weber kettle or a Big Green Egg, add some hickory smoke to the process.) The snags will crisp up and become golden and neatly grill marked – as you move them through 90 degrees after a few minutes and repeat the dose on the second side after a few more – before they are cooked.

Serve them with a dollop of tomato ketchup into which you have swirled plenty of Dijon mustard and eat them – not wrapped in disgusting supermarket white bread, please – before the main events of the barbecue, in your fingers.

And now, make a donation to a local charity if it makes you (and them) feel better. But never eat the sausages, which wallow in their own fat on vile hotplate devices, on offer at one of their confounded sausage sizzles.

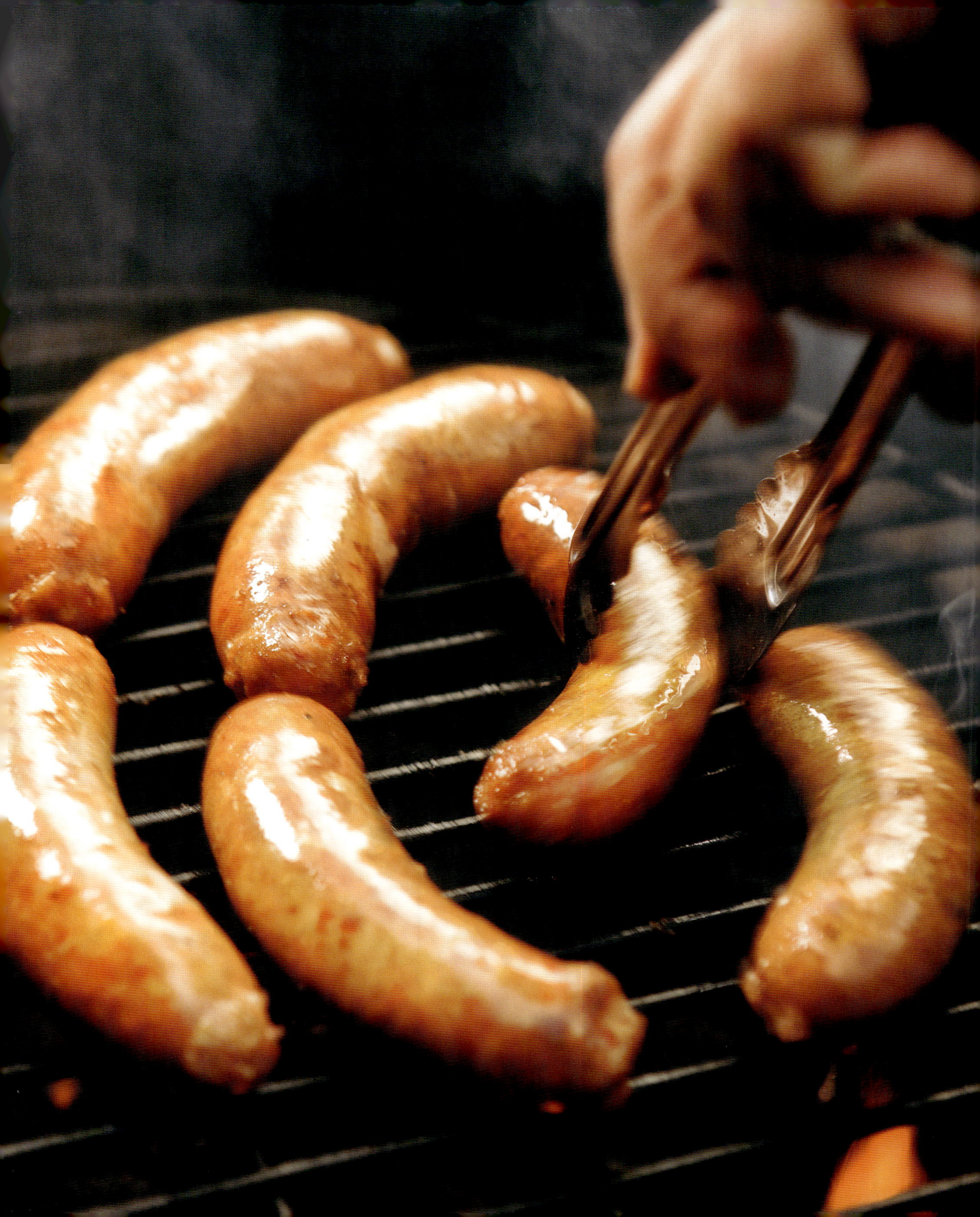

LAMB: the refined red meat

If there is nobility in beef, which there is of course, then there is elegance and refinement in lamb – a distinctively flavoured but infinitely more delicate red meat. And a meat, surely, that deserves to be handled with at least as much care and attention as we give to fine cuts of beef.

It is wonderfully versatile, and is the central ingredient of a wide range of food cultures. It is loved around the Mediterranean and down into the Middle East. The Greeks cook lambs on spits while Moroccans turn them into fragrant ragouts and finish their couscous over steam rising from pots of lamb stock. Indians base some fine curries on lamb. The French cook it magnificently while the British are inclined to overcook it, but adore it just the same. Americans, however, have never really understood lamb, and have certainly never grasped its potential as a barbecue meat. Which is odd.

This is one area of barbecue, however, in which we can teach them a thing or two. Because for one thing, the lamb available to us is far superior, and considerably cheaper, than anything Americans can buy. With this meat, I believe, we can make a real impact in world barbecue terms.

Starting right here…

BUTTERFLIED LEG: a Greek chorus

A carefully butterflied leg of lamb – have your butcher do it for you, and ask him to even out the thickness – is prime barbecue fare. It is even better if you marinate it, at least overnight, in a Greek combination of EV olive oil, garlic, oregano, crumbled fetta and lemon juice.

MARINADE:
EV OLIVE OIL
GARLIC
OREGANO
FETTA
LEMON JUICE

CIABATTA ROLLS OR TURKISH BREAD

HUMMUS

TZATZIKI OR GREEK GARLIC SAUCE

Roast your leg of lamb on a hot gas grill or, better still, over direct heat in a Weber kettle or Big Green Egg laced with wet hickory chips, covered, until barely cooked through – up to 20 minutes a side, depending on how well you like it cooked and how large the leg was to start with.

Never let the internal temperature rise above 55°C. Rest the meat, loosely tented, for 10 minutes before slicing it across the grain and serving slices on ciabatta rolls or on Turkish bread spread with hummus, perhaps, the lamb topped with a dollop of tzatziki, Greek garlic sauce, or whatever takes your fancy.

If you are adventurous, try a dollop of red currant jelly, and maybe a few coriander leaves, just to offend your dreary neighbours. Live a little, OK?

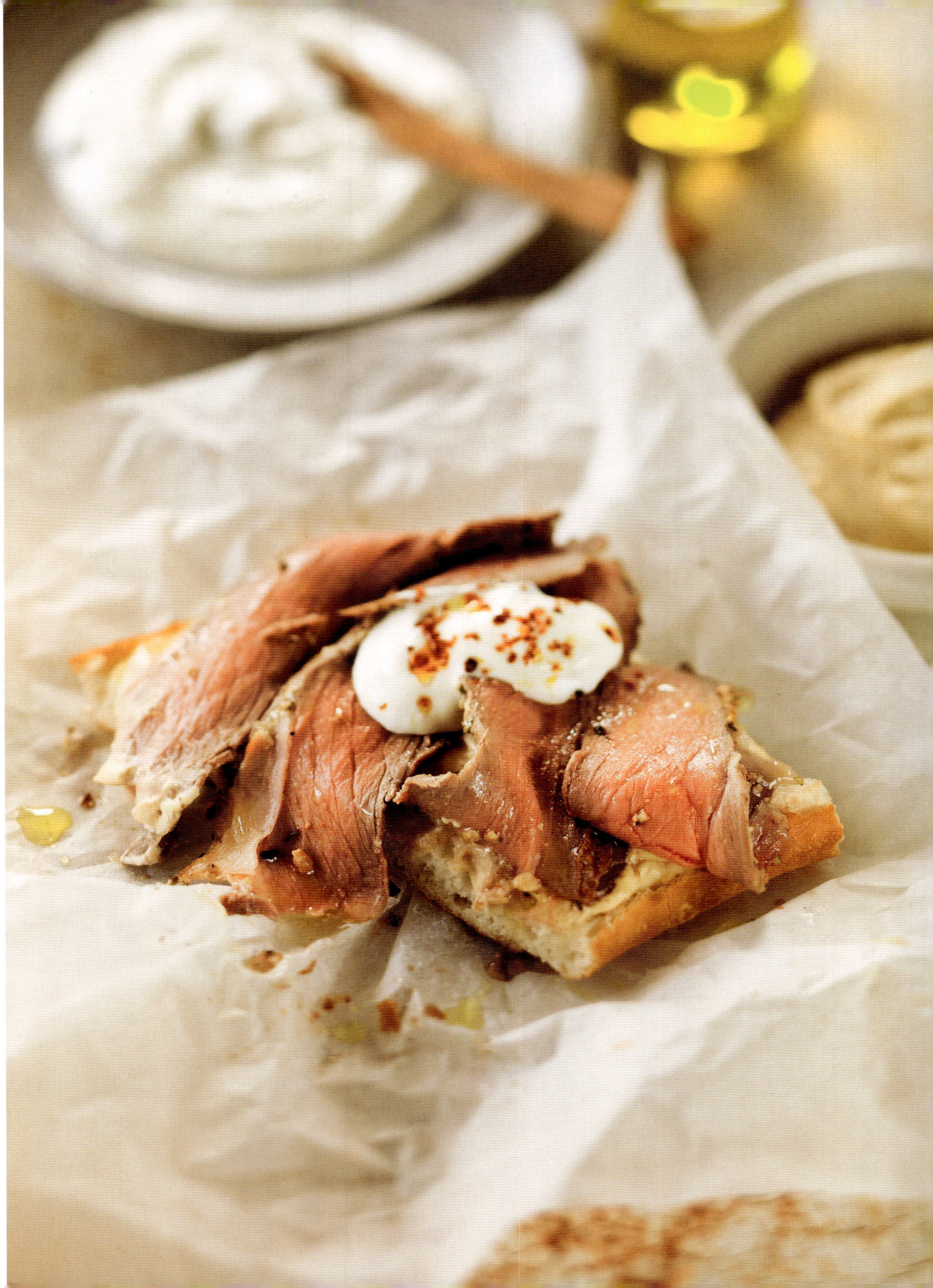

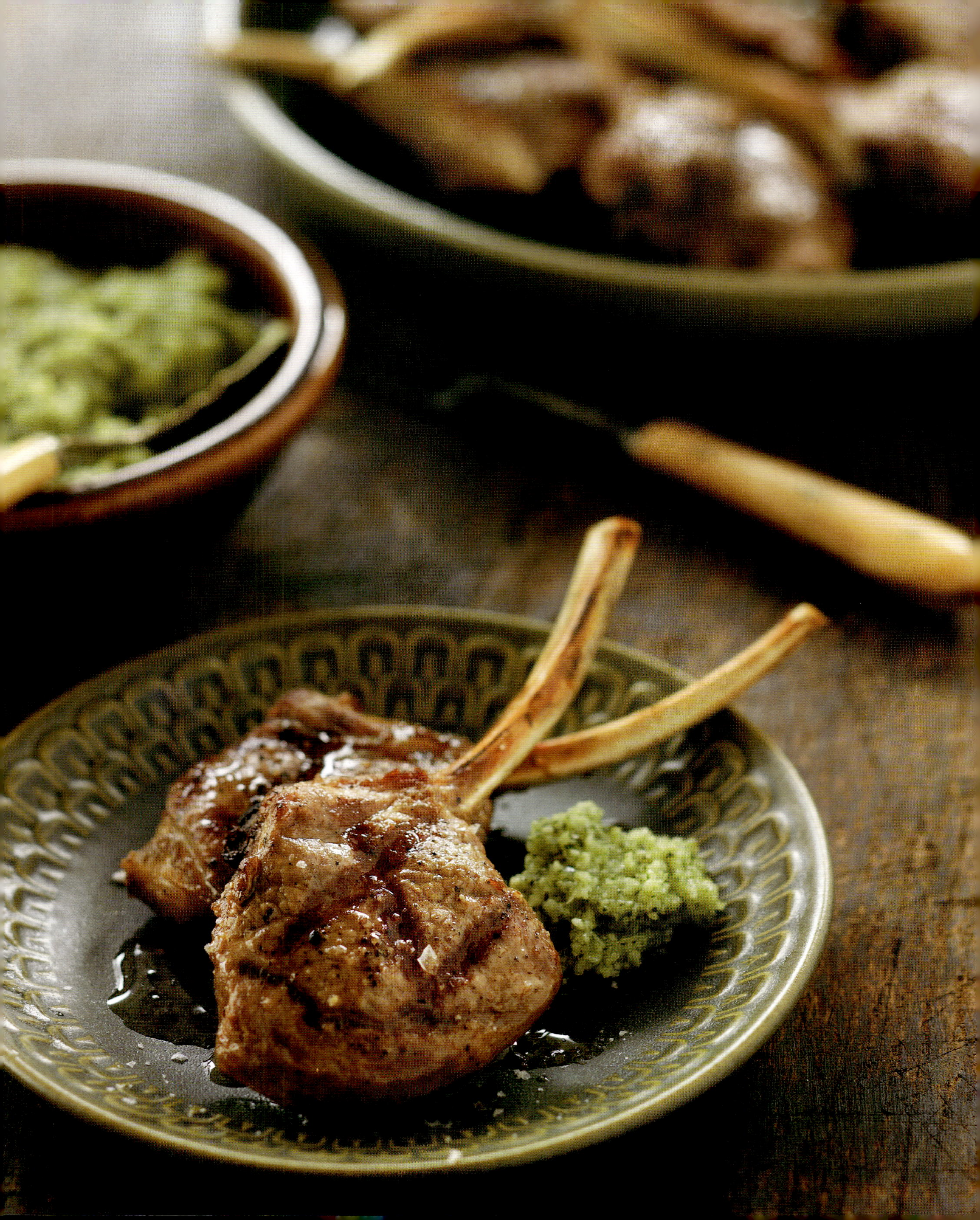

CUTLETS: in mint condition

Lamb cutlets, I suspect, are the most seriously abused of all barbecue meats in Australia – closely followed by dodgy sausages and mediocre steaks. And this is tragic.

LAMB CUTLETS
EV OLIVE OIL
SALT
PEPPER
CHIPOTLE SEASONING
MINT PESTO

Because a lamb cutlet is a glorious and luxurious piece of meat that requires very special attention. It is an ideal cut for gas grilling, although any grill on which you can achieve high cooking temperatures will do the trick.

Smoke, for once, is of little significance as the cooking time is brief. But achieving perfection in the matter of preparing lamb cutlets is every bit as important, in my view, as achieving the perfect steak. So with this in mind, try this:

Slice a couple of well-trimmed racks of lamb into cutlets and pound each cutlet just once to flatten it slightly. Or have your butcher do this for you.

Place these on a large plate, drizzle with EV olive oil and season with salt, pepper and a light sprinkle of chipotle (smoked chilli) seasoning such as Tone's (optional, but it makes the dish more interesting. Available from US, Spanish or Mexican suppliers).

Position the cutlets, in batches of not more than six at a time so you can watch the cooking time carefully, in the middle of the grill, and at 45 degrees to the grill bars. Drop the hood.

After a minute (exactly), turn each cutlet through 90 degrees. After another minute, flip each cutlet over and place at 45 degrees to the bars. And after another minute, turn through 90 degrees and cook for a final minute. And that's it. Get 'em off.

The cutlets will be pink, smoky and with glorious grill marks. Serve them with a dollop of mint pesto, and be reminded how good lamb can taste, and why it is not that expensive, really.

NOTE: Shoulder of lamb is a glorious cut of meat to barbecue and is at its best prepared, in a smoker, exactly as you would prepare a pork shoulder. But at the point where the pork shoulder is chopped and sauced, the lamb shoulder should simply be pulled apart into large chunks, garnished with salt, pepper and a squeeze of lemon, and served in generous chunks to be eaten, perhaps, with a tomato salad and crusty bread.

LAMB RIBLETS: same old routine, only better

The recognition of the brilliance of lamb ribs as barbecue fare is a very recent thing in Australia, much to our shame. But if pork ribs are the signature dish of US barbecue, perhaps lamb ribs should be ours.

LAMB RIBS

ALL-PURPOSE RUB

ALL-PURPOSE BARBECUE SAUCE

The rib racks from a lamb, inevitably, are smaller than those from a pig. But the amount of meat that clings to these tasty little blighters is truly remarkable.

The amount of fat is also impressive, which is one of the things preventing their wide acceptance. But by barbecuing them — and applying precisely the formula that delivers perfect smoky pork ribs — miracles can be worked.

Once again, you need a good butcher to prepare these for you, and to charge the very modest amount they should cost. Too many butchers toss them into the scrap bin to be sold as dog bones.

Which is ridiculous. Lamb ribs for dogs? Would that be served before or after the smoked salmon?

So, once you have obtained your lamb rib racks — or riblets, if your butcher insists — apply my all-purpose rub, place them in a resealable plastic bag, and refrigerate them overnight.

The next day, smoke them, over hickory or mesquite, at the usual smoking temperature — something not too far above 100ºC — for about 90 minutes. The Weber Smokey Mountain is the ideal barbecue for this, but a kettle with also do the trick.

Then, apply my all-purpose barbecue sauce liberally with a brush, double-wrap the ribs in foil and return them to the smoker for at least two hours more. That's it. Unwrap them, split the racks into individual ribs and serve with extra barbecue sauce.

And give the bloody dog a raw chicken neck, OK?

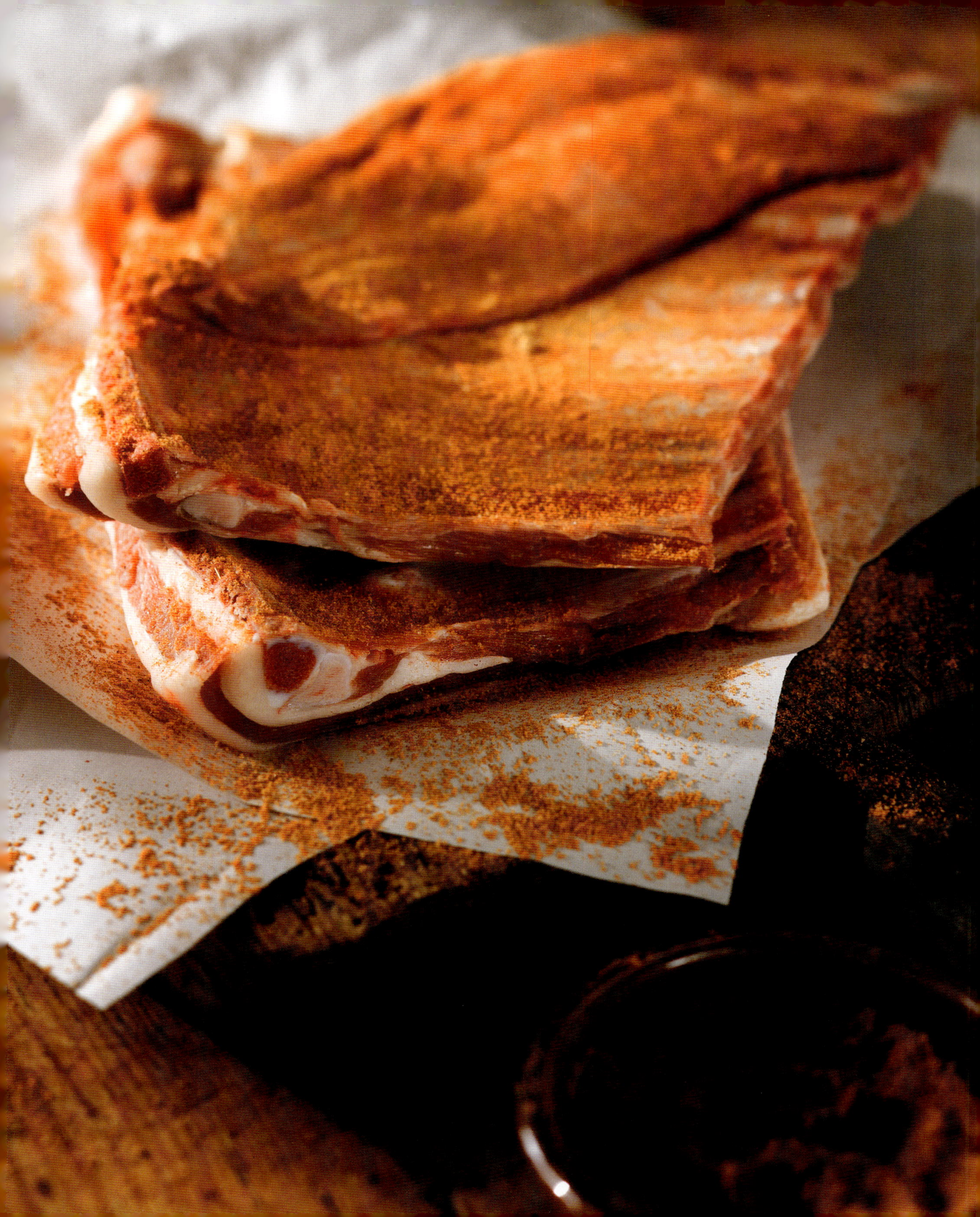

CHICKEN: stuff the Colonel doesn't know

In fact, stuff the Colonel, period. But, in fairness, at least he identified the chicken as a source of magnificent tucker. It's just that at that point, he rather lowered his sights...

The truth is that, apart from the pig, no animal is better suited to inspiring enlightenment and good will from your barbecue than the chicken.

It is a remarkable creature: built for roasting, cleverly designed to open out flat for grilling, suitably delicate for hot-smoking, divisible into splendid joints which satisfy very different requirements, and thoughtfully equipped with an orifice that accommodates a beer can. But more of that anon...

There are all sorts of ways of breathing extra life into a fit, healthy, free-range chook that, as illustrated by its athletic build, has lived a full, rewarding and active life. I am not, I confess, particularly impressed by organic chooks which have led, I suspect, rather sad little lives, and would have developed far more flavour had they been allowed out to scoff some free-range worms and neighbouring weeds through the fence. This, I need hardly point out, is purely a personal view.

Something that is beyond debate, however, is that a properly roasted free-range chook is just about the finest dish on the planet and one which, curiously, is more effortlessly executed on most barbecues than in an oven.

I like to roast a free-range chook – I like them around 2kg, or size 20 – in a Weber Q, which will cook one in no more than 75 minutes, and probably less.

The technique is simple: for a Q (and it works on a 120, a 220 or one of the brilliant 300s), place an oiled trivet down the centre of the grill over a double layer of foil of the same dimensions as the trivet. Remove the fat glands from just inside the cavity of the chook, rub the bird with EV olive oil and season well, inside and out.

Into the body cavity, place the remains of a lemon which you first squeeze over the bird, and a whisk made from a few good stems of parsley, a couple of bay leaves and a sprig or two of rosemary. And that's it.

When you oven-roast a bird, it's a good idea to turn it a quarter of a turn every 15 minutes or so. But in a barbecue, let nature take its course and leave the hood down and the bird undisturbed.

To ensure the bird does not roll around on the grill, I also use an adjustable roasting rack on top of the trivet (or, on a Weber kettle, a Big Green Egg or a larger gas barbecue such as a Weber Genesis, the rack without the trivet, but directly on top of a double strip of foil).

Your instant-read digital meal thermometer comes into play here: Lift the bird off the grill when the thickest part of the thigh registers an internal temperature of just above 70ºC and then rest the bird, loosely tented, for at least 10 minutes, and ideally 20 minutes, before carving.

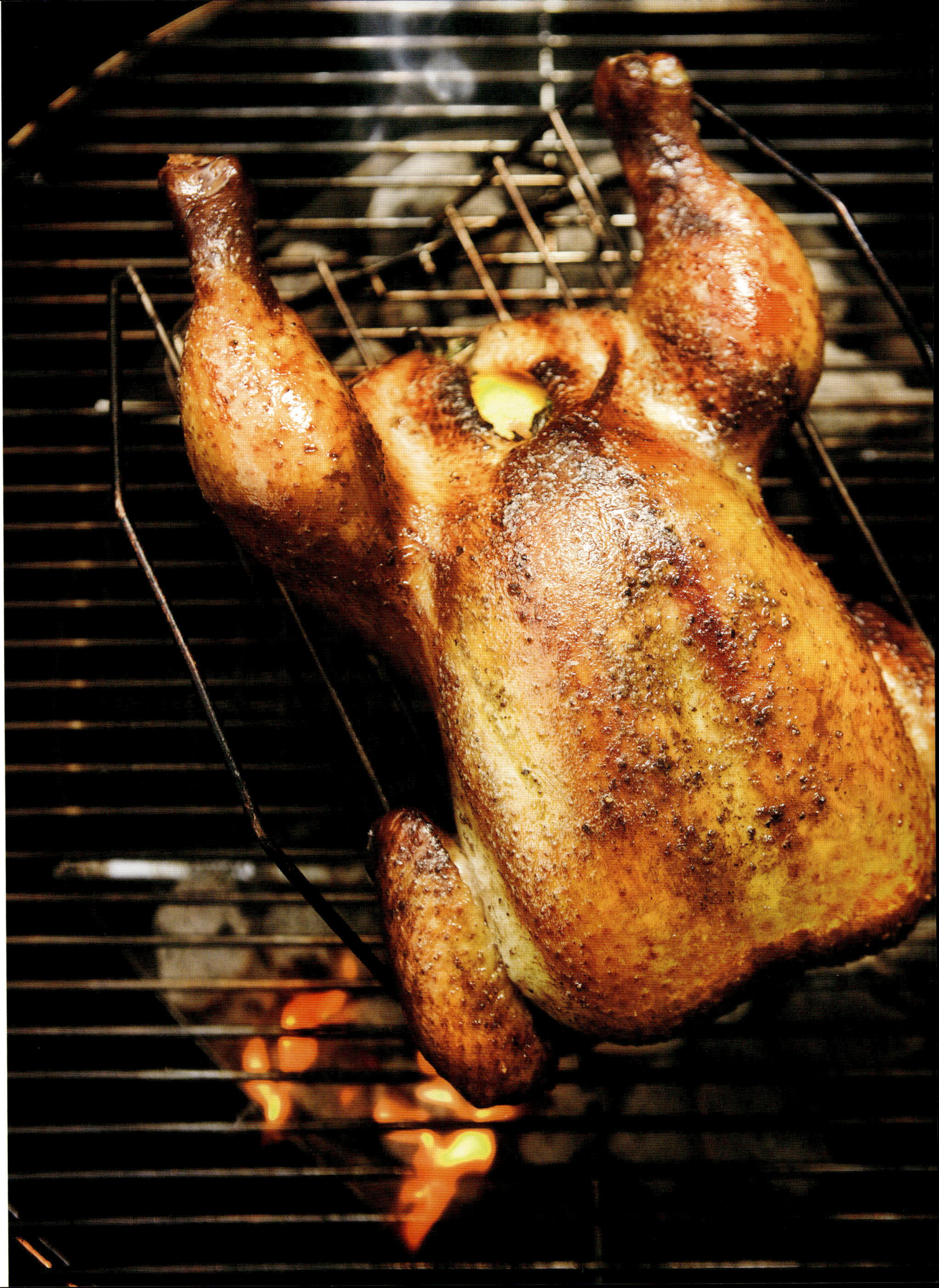

BEER-BUTT CHOOK: with consenting chickens

No barbecue tome would be complete without a thorough examination of one of the most popular, delicious and eye-catching barbecue creations of them all – a beer-butt chicken. Also called a beer-can chicken in polite society, but how much fun is polite society, anyway?

A WHOLE CHICKEN

A CAN OF BEER

BARBECUE RUB

GARLIC

The idea is simple enough: take a chicken and a can of beer. Drink a few glugs of the beer and insert the opened can up the clacker of the chicken. Stand the bird – using the two legs and the can as a tripod – in a covered barbecue in which it will cook, and smoke, to perfection, in a little over an hour, depending on the size of the chicken and the heat of the barbecue. Simple.

The technique originated in the US – probably in Tennessee. And there are a few refinements I recommend:

Using an old-fashioned beer can opener, put a few extra (triangular) holes in the top of the can before inserting.

If using a Weber kettle, cook the chicken in a drip tray on the bottom grill between the charcoal baskets. Use wood chips on the charcoal – I like hickory or apple wood with chicken – but not too much as it is a delicate meat. Loosely tented foil will prevent delicate parts of the bird from burning if you are cooking it at a lower level. While the Weber does a masterful job of this dish, as always, on this occasion a Big Green Egg is even better. Very few gas barbecues provide sufficient height to execute this dish. But maybe you could try it with a budgie and a thimble. Or maybe not.

Use my standard barbecue rub to prepare the chicken before cooking. Add some of the rub to the beer in the can and always add a flattened clove or two of garlic, also, to the can.

Lower the oiled and rubbed chicken – I use my preferred free-range birds of around 2kg – on to a wire holder gripping the opened can. Sit the bird, upright, on the grill. Cover the barbecue. Check for doneness (and an internal temperature of 70°C) after 1 hr 15 mins, but don't cook for more than 1 hr and 30 mins unless your barbecue is running a bit low on heat. Top up the coals in the Weber after the first hour if necessary, adding a few more wet wood chips, also.

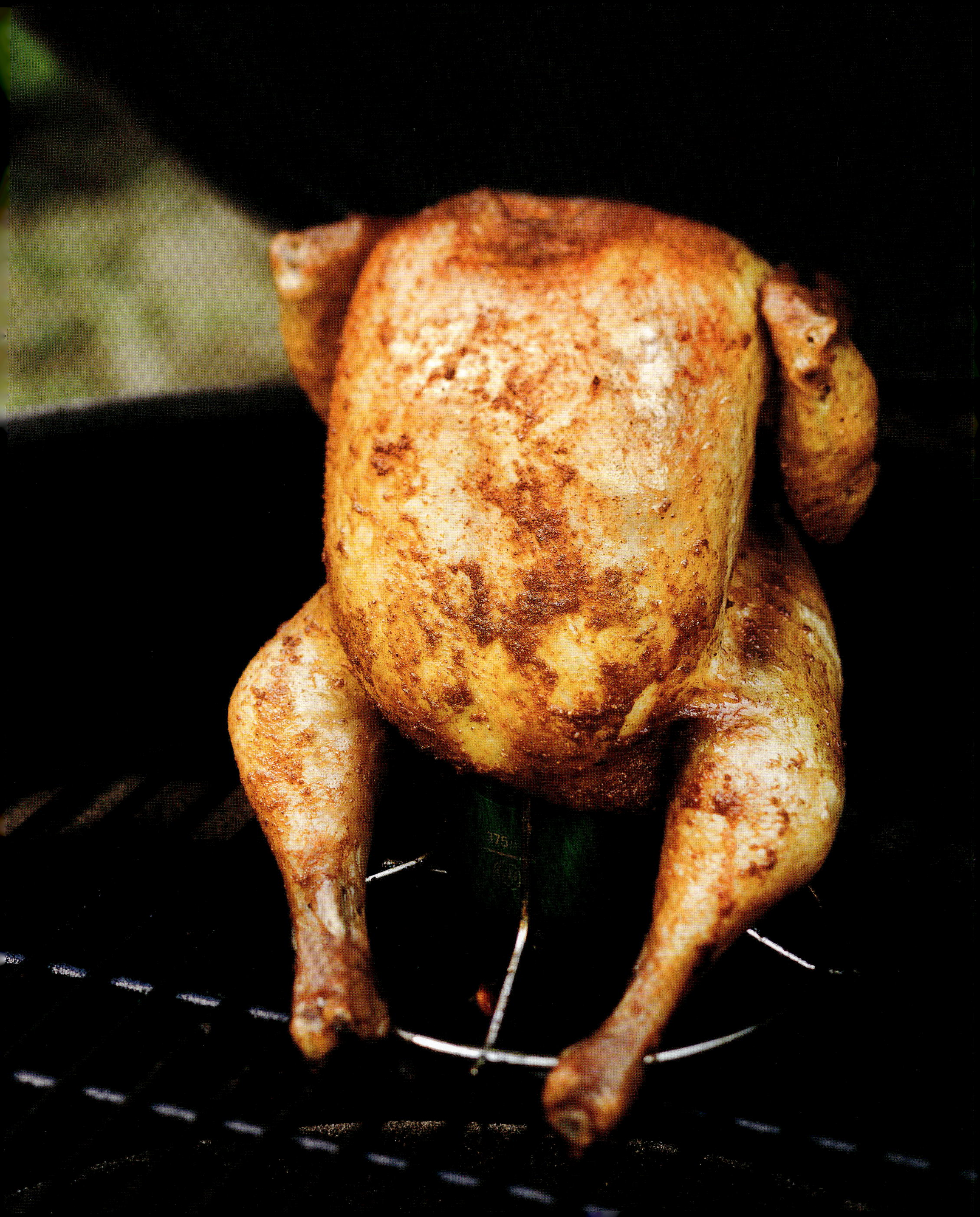

Now, the tricky bit: carefully lift the chicken, beer can still in place, using a couple of pairs of reliable tongs, on to a platter. Stand it upright and deliver it to the table for carving in this bizarre position, if you like. But remember, the beer will still be hot so do not spill it on yourself. Or your guests.

Do remember, however, to let your guests see how extraordinarily moist the chicken is when you make that first incision (to separate the marylands from the body).

NOTE: Simple wire holders for easing beer cans into consenting chickens and helping to hold them vertical are available from barbecue outlets, and are a good investment. But go for the simple ones rather than the elaborate jobs. While charcoal-powered barbecues are best for this dish, very large hooded gas barbecues will also do the job provided the hood is high enough. But the dish, unquestionably, is better in a barbecue which delivers real smoke. Different effects, also, can be achieved with different canned drinks, but I am suspicious of the claim that if you insert a can of Fanta into a duck and proceed as for beer-butt chicken, you will end up with a passable duck *à l'orange*.

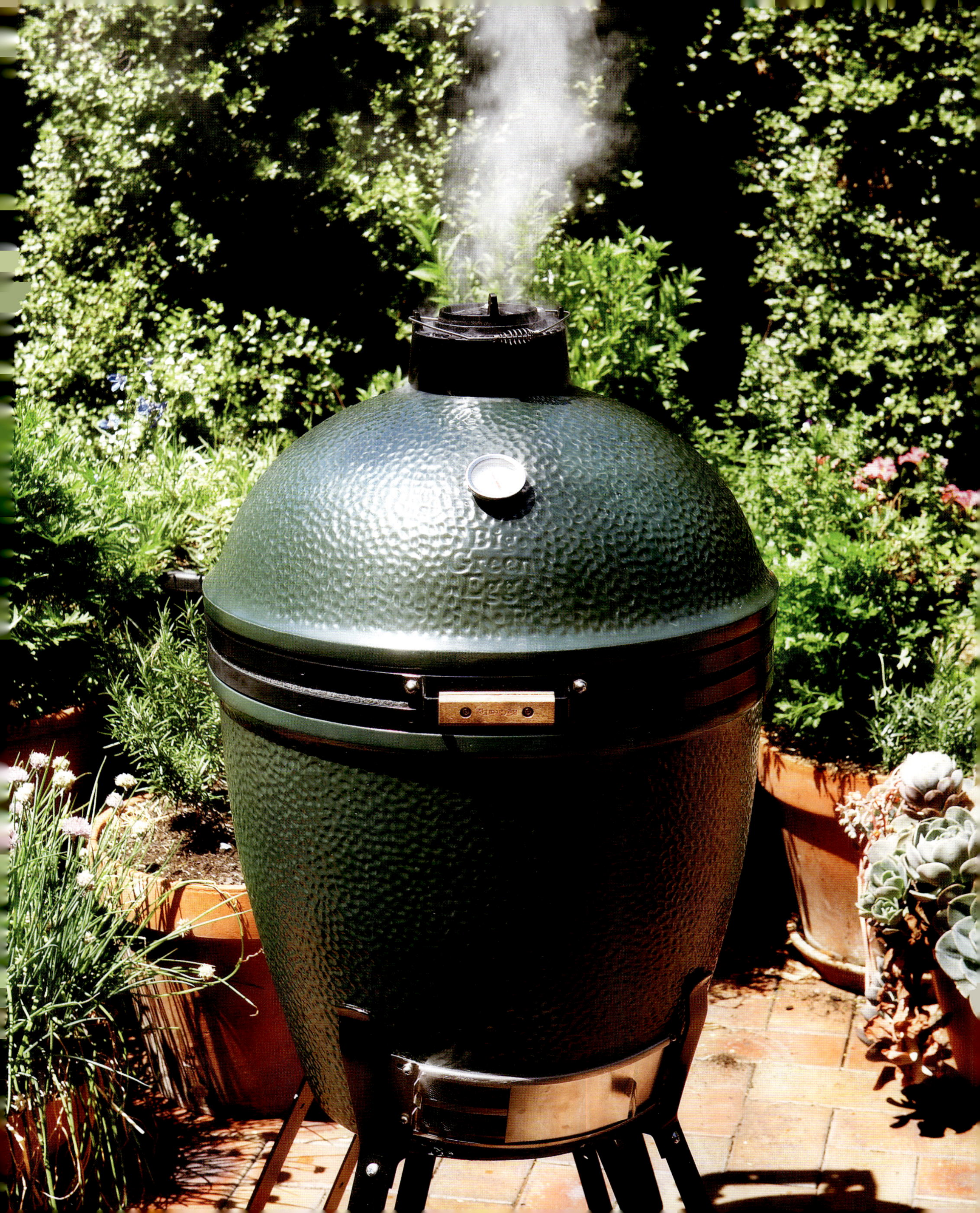

BIRD OR BUTTERFLY: more chicken magic

Portuguese chicken is a dish that has been made popular in Melbourne by the legendary Jonathan's of Collingwood, a butcher shop that has become something of a shrine for devout carnivores and fanatical barbecuers.

LARGE BUTTERFLIED FREE-RANGE CHOOK

2 TBS ALL-PURPOSE RUB

1 TBS PAPRIKA

A PINCH OF CINNAMON

Because at Jonathan's, they butterfly large free-range chooks, apply their Portuguese rub, which contains paprika and cinnamon and a couple of things they may not tell you about, and that's it.

Place one of these – either a Jonathan's original, or your own version which you can make by adding an additional tablespoon of paprika and a good pinch of cinnamon to 2 tbs of my all-purpose rub, and applying it generously to the skin of a chicken you have split down the backbone – or, better still, down either side of the backbone, which you then remove – and cook it over indirect heat. My preferred method is on a Weber kettle, over a foil tray of water, with a sprinkle of wet hickory chips on each basket of coals. Around 20-25 minutes a side should do the trick, but check the thigh temperature with an instant-read digital thermometer if you are unsure.

A brilliant variation of the butterflied chook, however, can be achieved with spatchcocks or poussins – one per person – which should be split down the back, salted and then brushed, before cooking, with my diavola sauce, which I make as follows:

Heat 4 minced garlic cloves, 2 tsp ground black pepper and 2 tsp chilli flakes in ¼ cup EV olive oil until the garlic sizzles. Remove from the heat and allow to cool. That's it. Don't overcook spatchcocks: around 10-12 minutes per side should be plenty. If you end up loving the diavola treatment as much as I do, try it on larger butterflied chickens, or even on smaller birds, notably quail. Even fat, farmed ones come to life with a splash of this oil.

While we are on the subject of these delectable and widely misunderstood little birds, they are worthy of some serious attention by grillmasters everywhere. Simply split a dozen or so down the backbone, or on either side of the backbone which you can remove, along with the neck and the tiny pope's nose. Brush them with a basic Asian marinade of soy, honey, ginger and garlic, and grill them, ideally with smoke but a gas grill also works well, for about 10 minutes a side. Serve them, jointed, as finger food.

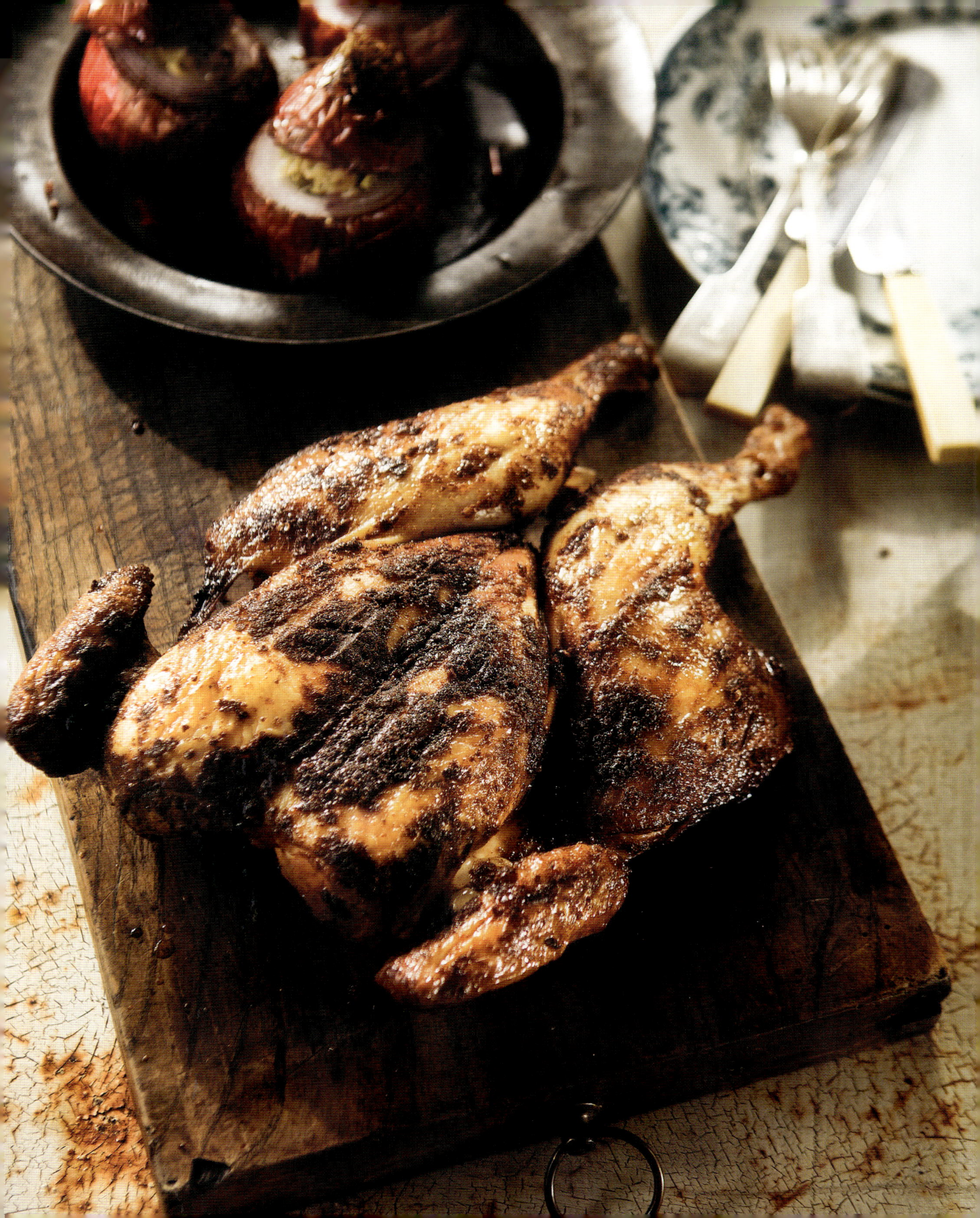

GRILLED DUCK BREASTS: it's in the glaze

Duck is another meat that responds admirably to cooking over live fire. A whole roasted bird is magnificent, obviously – simply cooked, on an adjustable roasting rack, over indirect heat, swathed in hickory smoke, and on a Weber kettle.

2 DUCK BREASTS

125G BUTTER

½ CUP DARK RUM

1 TBS CIDER VINEGAR

½ CUP DARK BROWN SUGAR

3 TBS DIJON MUSTARD

½ TBS GROUND CLOVES

½ TBS GROUND CINNAMON

SALT

PEPPER

But duck breasts, also, are very special, and accumulate a remarkable amount of rich, charred flavour when grilled, fiercely, over charcoal – again, with hickory smoke.

Try this: Make a sweet glaze by melting 125g of butter with ½ cup of dark rum. Stir in ½ cup of dark brown sugar, 3 tbs Dijon mustard, 1 tbs cider (apple or pear) vinegar, ½ tsp each of ground cloves and ground cinnamon, salt and pepper to taste. Simmer until reduced to a syrup (5-6 minutes).

Take two duck breasts (for two people). Prick the skin of each with a fork or slice lengthways with a Stanley knife, coat with EV olive oil and season well. Then, place on a very hot ribbed grill, skin side down. Try a Weber kettle or a Big Green Egg and cook over direct heat. Or, even better – fire up a Weber Go-Anywhere with a hardwood charcoal, toss on some wet hickory chips and try this approach on your next enlightened picnic or camping trip.

Place the breasts on the grill at 45 degrees to the grill bars and, after about 4 minutes, move through 90 degrees and cook for another 4 minutes to achieve a lattice of deep, dark grill marks as the fat drains from the bird. Turn, and repeat the exercise, cooking covered at all times.

After you have turned the breasts the first time, brush the skin with the glaze. Then, turn again, brush the bottom with the glaze, turn again and re-glaze the skin side. Remove from the heat and rest, loosely tented in foil, for 5-10 minutes in a warm place, or until cooked to your liking. Slice across the grain, brush with more of the glaze and serve.

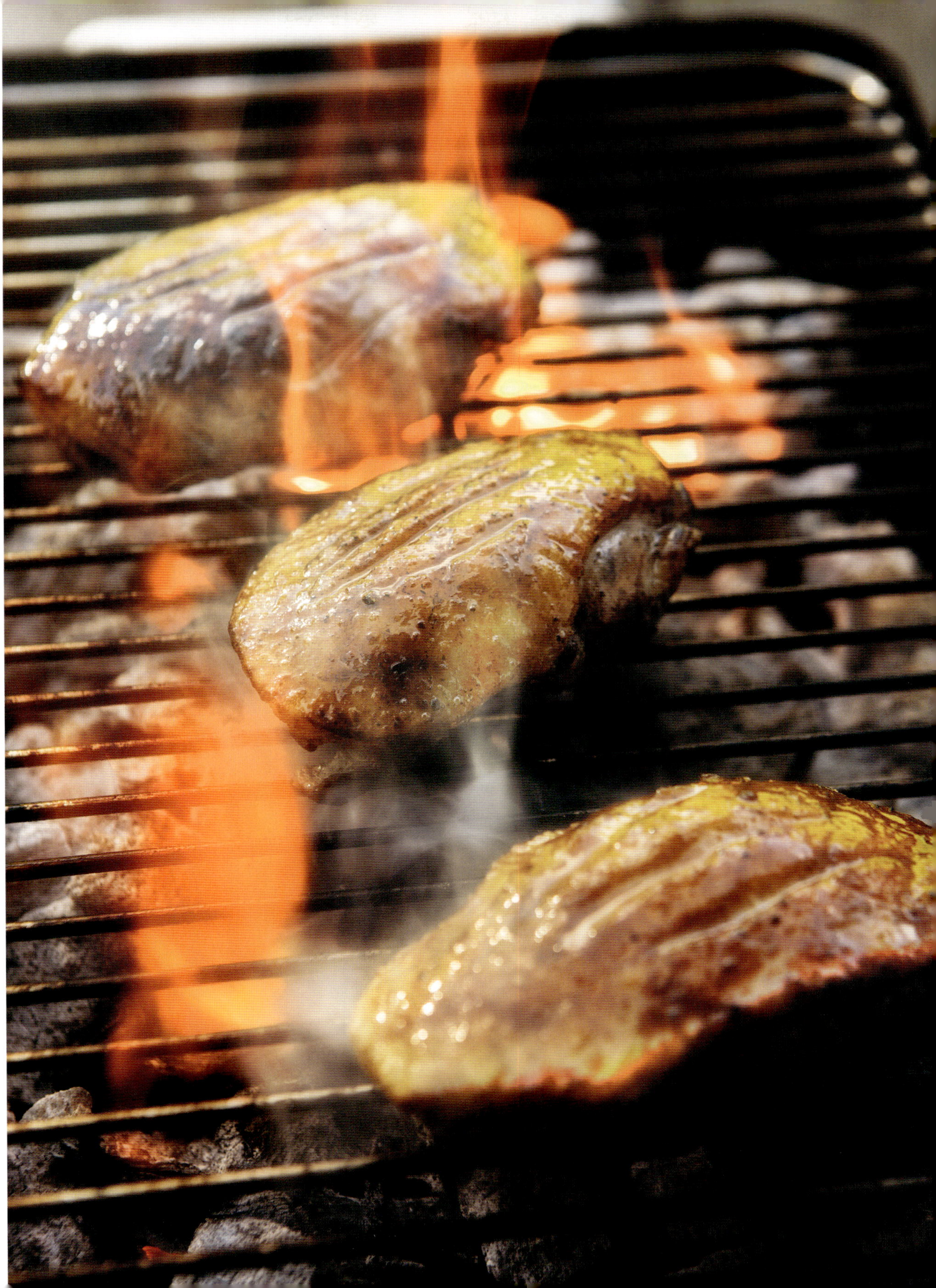

VEGETABLES

VEGIE MAGIC: and yes, I am serious

The very idea of vegetarians rolling up for a barbecue is cause for great mirth in certain circles. But not in this one. Because simple, grilled vegetables, and any number of outstanding vegetarian dishes, make excellent barbecue fare – even for devout carnivores.

Like fine cuts of meat, vegetables respond brilliantly to being generously coated in EV olive oil, well seasoned and seared on a blisteringly hot grill. Handsome grill marks can improve the experience – depending, of course, upon the vegetable.

Some vegies may need a little extra encouragement before they can be persuaded to deliver of their best: baby carrots, for example, respond well to a glaze of melted butter, orange juice and maple syrup, before and after grilling.

So, experiment: in the case of more substantial vegetables – pumpkins and sweet potatoes come to mind – the best results come from more substantial chunks or wedges which can be started in the way outlined here, but may then need extra time, over indirect heat or even on the resting rack of a gas barbecue, or over the cool part of a two-level fire in a Weber kettle, to collect their thoughts and achieve an appropriate level of opulence – helped along with a generous allocation of butter when you serve them.

And let's not forget the wonder of starting a large, floury potato roasting well before the meat – washed, but not in foil, ever – on a quiet corner of the grill. Because with grated cheese, sour cream, chives and one or two other things, an entire vegetarian meal – entire by vegie standards, at any rate – can be constructed around a smokily roasted spud.

So, sit your vegie friends in a corner and ignore them, if you must. But at the very least, you can feed the poor blighters...

CORN AND ASPARAGUS: who'd have thought?

Start your vegetarian barbecue adventures simply with two vegies – corn and asparagus – that are exquisitely suited to the grill. There are, quite simply, no better first courses or side dishes than these.

FRESH ASPARAGUS
EV OLIVE OIL
BLACK PEPPER
SEA SALT
CHIPOTLE MAYONNAISE

Try this:

First, asparagus – fresh, seasonal, green stalks. Snap the stems and discard the bases or toss them into a stockpot if you have one on the go. Wash and dry what's left.

Now, fire up and prepare a grill – gas or charcoal – for high, direct cooking. Thoroughly oil and season the asparagus with EV olive oil, freshly ground black pepper and sea salt and position them on the grill, perpendicular to the grill bars.

After just over a minute, turn them through a third of a turn and lower the hood. Repeat this after another minute or so. Then give them just a touch longer in any position and lift off the grill on to a serving platter. Let them cool slightly, then offer them around with a dip of chipotle mayo (page 14).

Other vegetables worth grilling – simply by cutting into rings or splitting lengthways, coating generously with EV olive oil and seasoning well – include pumpkin, eggplant, zucchinis, turnips, parsnips, sweet potatoes, fennel, witlof and, my favourite, radicchio.

In all cases, slice or simply split, brush with EV olive oil, season and grill, turning once on each side through 90 degrees, to achieve perfect grill marks, until cooked through.

Grilled vegies are even better served with a splash of chimichurri (page 12). After all, even vegetarians deserve a little excitement in their sad little lives. (Just kidding ... sort of.)

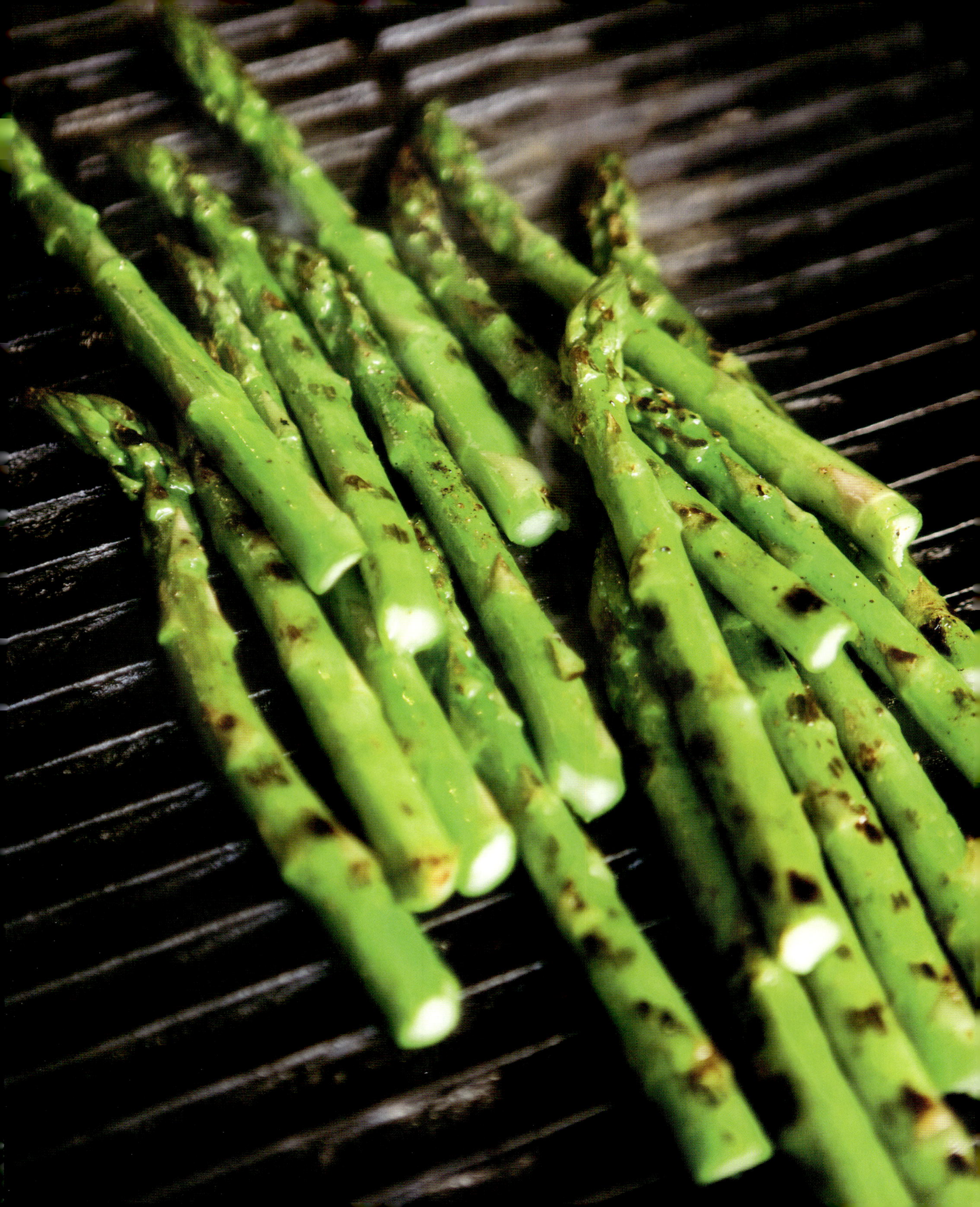

ROASTED CHILLI CORN: feel the earth move

When my summer barbecue classes wind up late on Saturday afternoons, we usually take a vote to decide on our favourite dish of the day. There are always plenty of votes for this one – an unorthodox approach, based on freshly roasted corn I first tasted outside a Mexican supermarket in Houston, but even better.

FRESH CORN (WITH HUSKS)

CHIPOTLE MAYONNAISE

PARMESAN

Have that chipotle mayo handy and grate (on a microplane grater, which keeps it very light) a generous slab of good Italian parmesan (ideally, reggiano). Now, peel back the husks of as many cobs of corn as you plan to serve and leave them attached to the cob. If you have done it correctly, each will look like an adman's ponytail, and will make excellent handles for the corn. Remove and discard any silk from the cobs.

Still using a hot grill set for direct grilling, position the cobs – neither oiled nor seasoned on this occasion – on the grill, perpendicular to the grill bars, and with the husks protruding from the hood when you lower it.

After a minute and a half raise the hood, turn the cobs through a quarter of a turn by twisting the ponytails, and lower the hood.

Do this each minute for about 6-8 minutes, or until the cobs are golden and flecked with blackened kernels. Lift the cobs off the grill and on to a platter.

To serve the corn, brush each hot cob with the chipotle mayo and sprinkle with parmesan. And no, don't think too hard about it before you have tasted it.

Because you are about to be amazed…

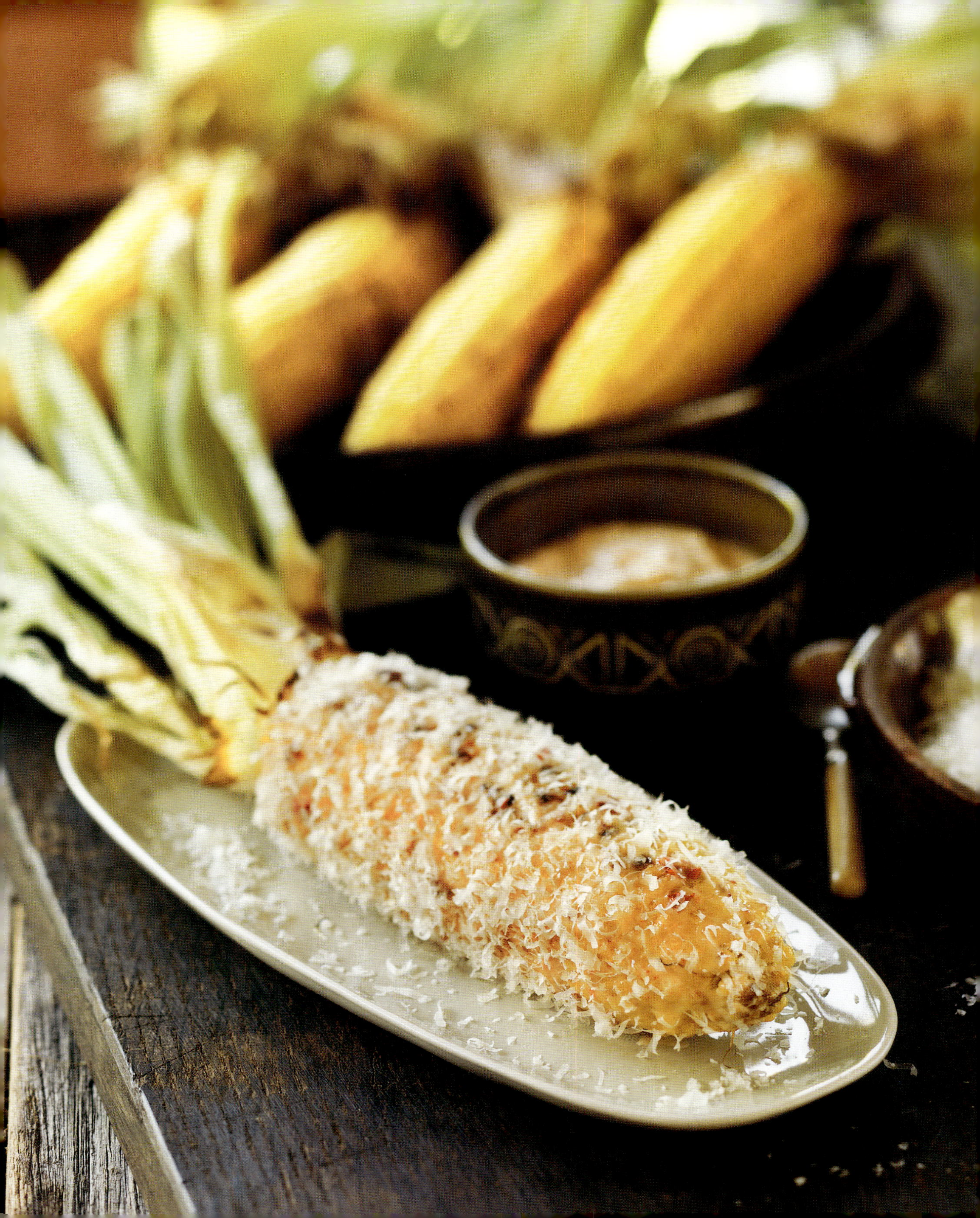

MUSHROOMS: the legendary mushie burger(s)

Big, flat mushrooms, especially fresh ones which are very moist, are brilliant barbecue fare, and are at the heart of the burger that has become something of a Melbourne legend: I serve these, every Saturday, at Melbourne's Prahran market, and they are starting to pop up elsewhere, which is flattering.

12 LARGE FLAT MUSHROOMS

PARSLEY BUTTER

CIABATTA ROLLS

CHIPOTLE MAYONNAISE

SALAD ONIONS

PARMESAN

To make them, simply brush half a dozen large flat mushrooms clean (a moist Chux does a great job of this), remove most of each stem, oil and season both sides of each mushroom and place them, gill sides down, on a hot grill.

After about 90 seconds, turn them through 90 degrees. After another 90 seconds, flip them over. After 90 seconds, place a disc of parsley butter (page 12) in each mushroom, turn them through 90 degrees, and lower the hood.

They will be cooked in another two minutes and the butter will have begun to melt into them. Lift off the grill on to a platter and place to one side.

Prepare a small ciabatta roll (or divide up a ciabatta loaf) for each mushroom by splitting and warming them on the grill – for about 20 seconds, crust sides down, and another 20 seconds cut sides down. Lift them off and spread all cut sides with chipotle mayo.

Place a mushroom, gill sides up, on each base, top with slices of salad onion and then sprinkle generously with grated parmesan. Replace the top of each bun.

Eat. Pray. Marvel.

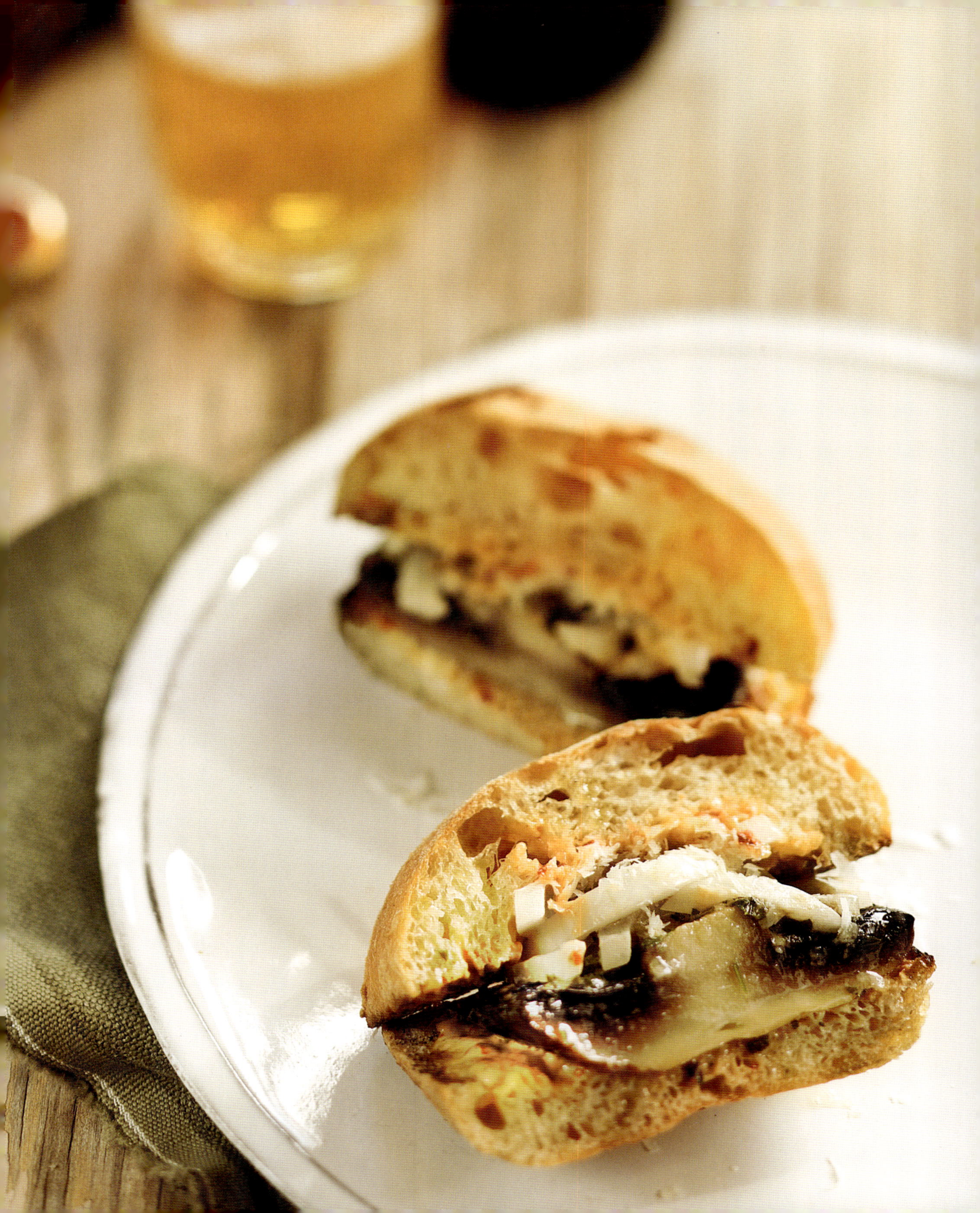

the legend grows...

Now that's a great dish. And pretty simple, provided you nail the components. But for a slightly more complex variation, and a dish that dips even more deeply into the magic of chipotle chillies, try this spectacular variation.

Start with those large field mushrooms – one per person, and ciabatta rolls, likewise. But this time, make a marinade by blending 3 chillies and 1 tsp of the adobo sauce with 3 cloves of garlic, 1 small red onion, 3 tbs balsamic vinegar, ½ cup olive oil, salt and pepper.

Wipe clean as many mushrooms as you need and slosh this marinade into the gill sides. Let them marinate for 2-3 hours, and then grill them on a covered, hot barbecue, gill sides down, for about 2 minutes (and yes, it's messy, but worth it). Flip the mushrooms, adding the rest of the marinade to the gill sides, now facing upwards, of the mushrooms. After another two minutes, turn each mushroom through 90 degrees and top each with a slice of comté (French gruyère) cheese or similar, which will begin to melt into the mushroom in a minute or two.

Split and lightly grill your ciabattas as in the previous recipe. Lift the mushrooms off the grill and position them on the bottoms of the ciabatta rolls. Top each mushroom with slices of fresh avocado, season the avocado, replace the tops of the roll and eat. With a very cold beer. And a few appreciative words of Spanish, OK?

RED ONIONS: stuff 'em, roast 'em

While we are on the subject of spectacular vegetables, equally impressive are large, red onions, stuffed and roasted on the grill, ideally with hickory smoke...

Try this:

Slice the top off each onion, about a third of the way down from the root end and scoop a generous cavity into the bottom section. Retain these scrapings and chop them.

Mix them with breadcrumbs, grated gruyère cheese and work in a knob of your parsley herb butter. Stuff each onion with this mixture and replace the tops.

Cook these – as you would the stuffed, smoked pears opening the next section of the book – on foil haloes, until they are soft to the touch.

Serve with just about anything of a meaty nature, especially roasted meats.

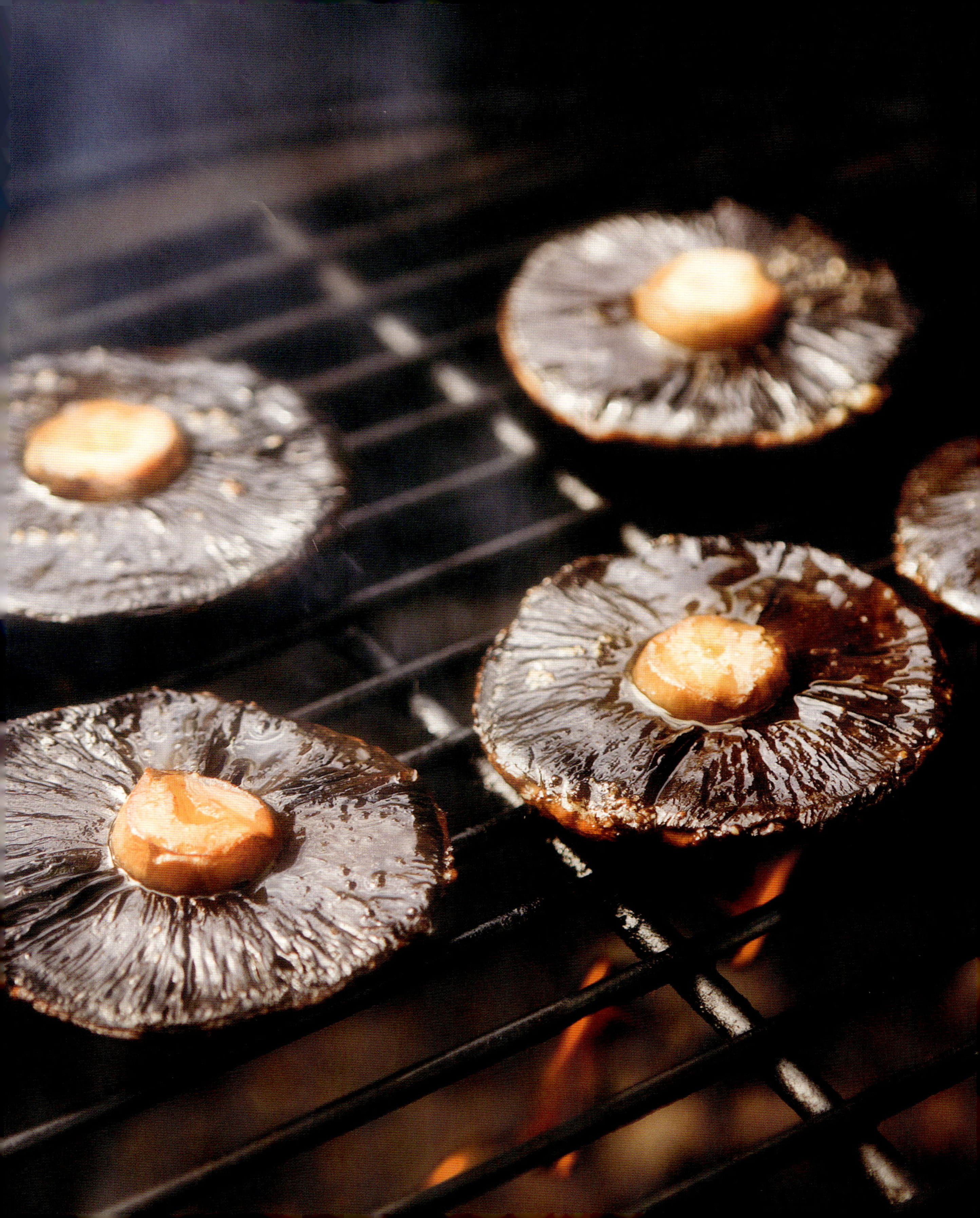

GLOBE ARTICHOKES: at home in the flames

Something very special happens when you introduce fresh globe artichokes to hot coals. Try it and see:

GLOBE ARTICHOKES

GARLIC BUTTER

Trim the stems of the artichokes to around 2cm from the bottom of the globe, and trim another 2cm or so off the top of each artichoke. Fire up a charcoal barbecue, this time with hardwood charcoal and not charcoal briquettes.

I love to use a Weber Go-Anywhere for this job, and serve the artichokes as unorthodox picnic treats. Simply press each artichoke, stem first, down into the coals, mounding them up slightly if necessary.

Cook them until a long, sharp fork or skewer tells you they are cooked through – timing will vary hugely with each barbecue, and due to the size and freshness of the artichokes.

When they are ready, lift them out, let them cool slightly, place them on a cutting board and split each of them lengthways. If there is a choke, remove it, along with the charred, outer leaves.

Then, simply drizzle the warm artichokes with melted garlic butter and eat them in your fingers. Or allow them to cool and serve them with a vinaigrette.

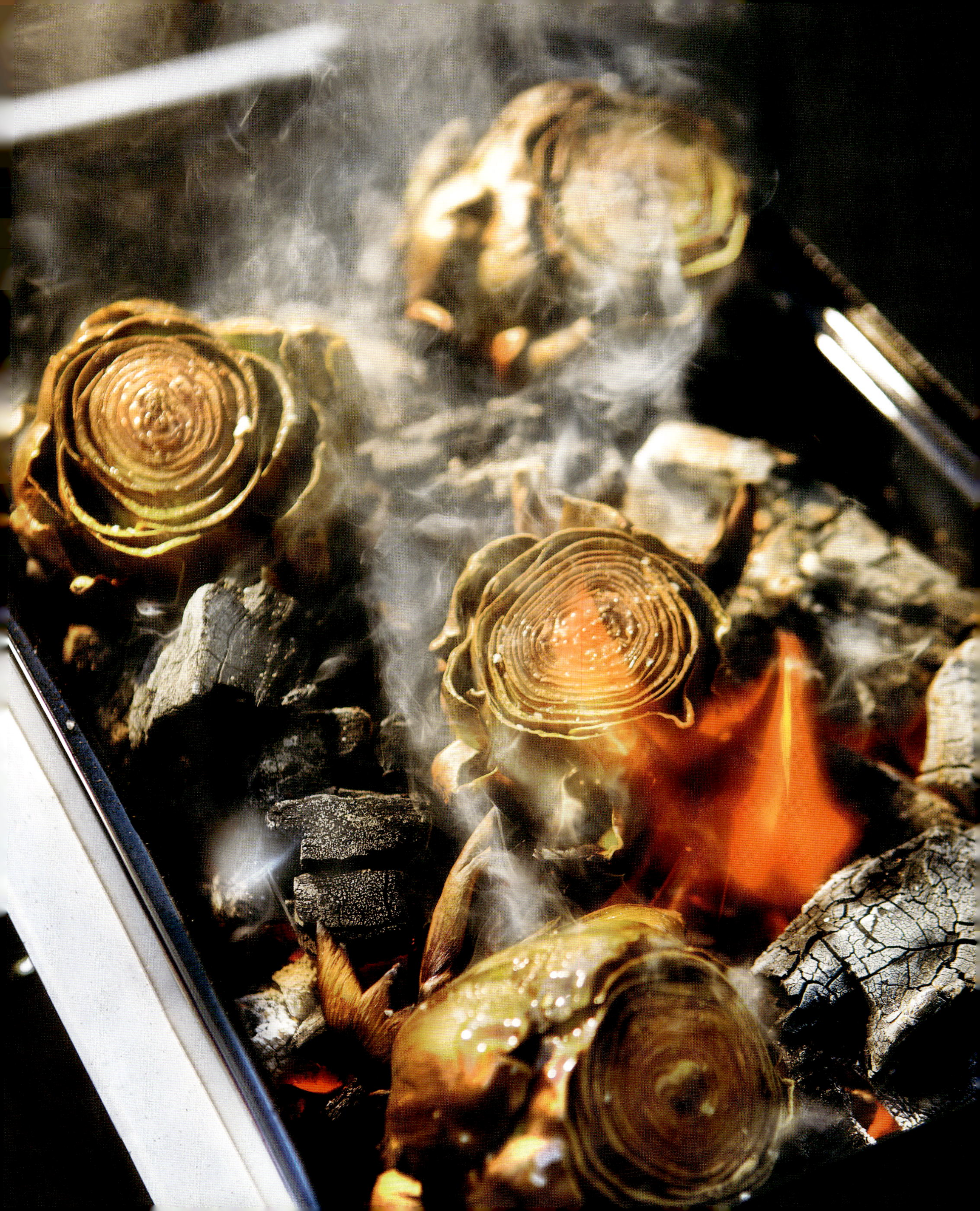

FRUIT

ROASTED FRUIT: smoky, happy endings

It is essential, I believe, to end every barbecued meal as you began it — by serving something delectable that is produced through the appropriate application of heat and smoke. My favourite barbecue desserts invariably involve fruit which has been roasted, grilled and/or smoked. Or even, when times are tough and fuel is low, eaten raw. Which means never, of course.

For all sorts of reasons, largely to do with the sugar content of most fruit, wondrous things happen when the flesh of fruit comes into contact with extreme heat. In some cases, with stone fruit and mangoes for example, it is simply a matter of placing the cut surfaces on a clean, hot grill, turning them after they have been suitably grill-marked and applying raw sugar while you cook them skin side down.

While in other cases — with pears and apples, for example — a more considered and slightly more elaborate approach is called for. This generally involves stuffing the fruit. By which, of course, I do not mean cooking it until it explodes or collapses.

Treat fruit with the same sort of respect you apply to meat, and you will be suitably rewarded. And in addition to that, a barbecued fruit masterpiece will, for the second time in the same day, etch a smile into the pinched features of that vegetarian friend we were talking about...

ASIAN ROASTED PEARS: send 'em packham

If I had to choose a favourite barbecued dessert, it would be my Asian roasted pears – a barbecued extrapolation of a classical French dessert called poires à la chinoise in which pears are peeled, stuffed and gently braised in white wine before being served with a syrup made on the pan juices.

4 PACKHAM PEARS

SULTANAS

4 TBS HONEY

GINGER SYRUP

PINE NUTS

CRÉME FRAÎCHE

My grillmaster's version is a more rustic affair, but utilises some of the same ingredients to achieve a distinctly Asian leaning. It's a magical dessert which, finished over hickory smoke, is even more enchanting than the original.

Try this:

Take four packham pears (the thin skin and succulence of a ripe packham makes this the essential variety for the dish). Leave unpeeled but slice off a cap about 2cm down from the base of the stem of each and, using a melon-baller, dig out the core and seeds, and some of the surrounding flesh, taking care not to break through the bottoms.

Chop a handful of sultanas with a handful of pine nuts, and warm 4 tbs of honey so it runs easily. Stuff the pears loosely with the sultana mixture and drizzle in the honey, dividing the fillings between the four pears. Now, take a quantity of the syrup from a jar of ginger in syrup and drizzle a little into each pear. Replace the caps.

Tear four square pieces of foil, loosely roll each square diagonally into a cylinder and then twist it into a circle, rather like a halo, and compress it slightly. Each pear will sit on the grill, securely, pressed down into one of these.

Sit the pears on their shiny little foil seats on the grill of a charcoal or gas barbecue – my preferred device for the job is a Big Green Egg, fired up with briquettes and laced with wet hickory chunks. Roast the pears until they become tender, which will take around 20-30 minutes, depending upon the ripeness of the fruit.

Lift the pears off the grill and lower each into a serving bowl. Tip the caps to one side and top each pear with pouring cream or *crème fraîche*. And if there is a finer end to a barbecued meal than that, please, send me the recipe.

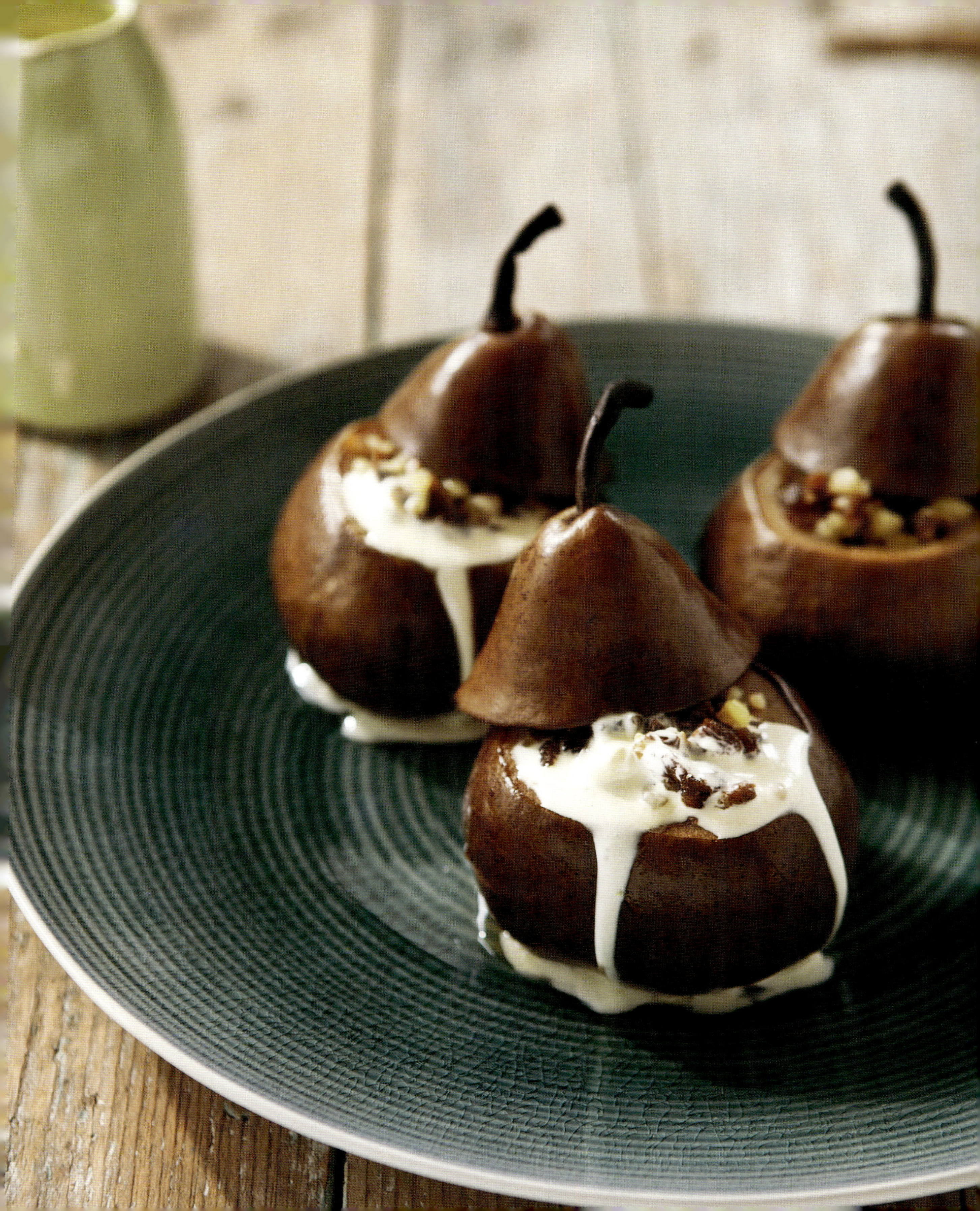

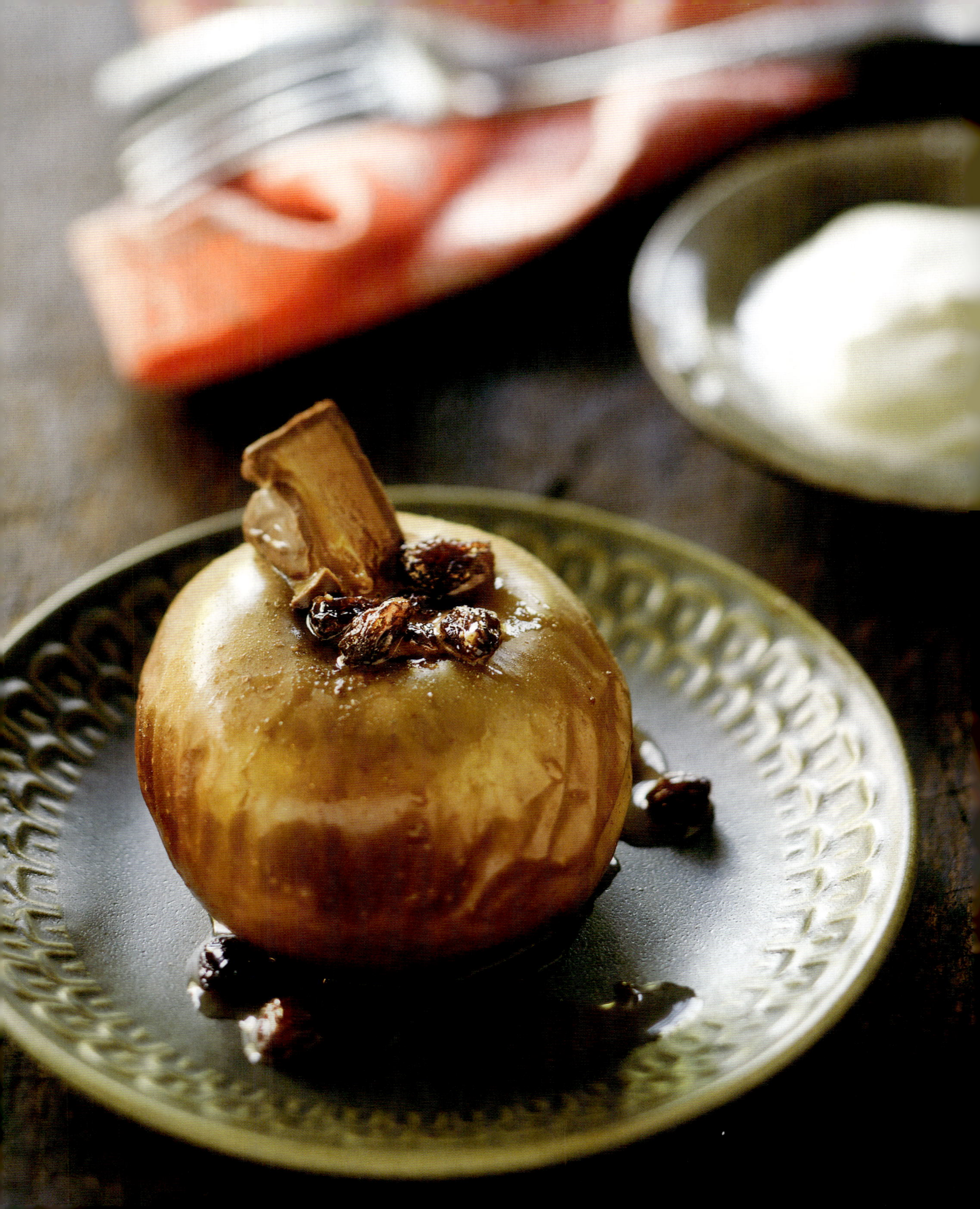

MARS BARS APPLES: silly but wonderful

Take four fuji apples – the variety is important, I promise you, but if fujis are unavailable, golden delicious apples will do the job, while granny smiths, curiously, will not.

4 FUJI APPLES

2 MARS BARS

DARK BROWN SUGAR

SULTANAS

LIQUEUR MUSCAT

DOUBLE CREAM

Use a corer to remove the core from each apple. Then, slice the bottom 1cm from each core and replace it in the apple to serve as a plug. Now, sit each apple on a small square of foil and fold it half-way up the apple, all the way around, to reinforce the seal made by the bottom of the core.

Coarsely chop a couple of Mars Bars and drop pieces into each apple, to fill each of them, loosely, to about half-way up. Add some dark brown sugar and a few sultanas to each apple, and top up, loosely, with more Mars Bar pieces. Finally, pour in enough liqueur muscat just to spill over the top edges of each apple, create four more of those foil halos we discussed in the pear recipe, and sit an apple in each, on the grill.

Cook these, ideally on a Weber kettle or a Big Green Egg with plenty of hickory smoke, until the apples soften. Time will vary but start checking (by squeezing) after 20-30 minutes, although it may take longer than that. Remove each apple to a small bowl, drizzle with double cream, and accompany with a small glass of that liqueur muscat.

The pattern emerging here, clearly, is for fruit into which additional flavours are imparted, cooked over heat and smoke. Stone fruit are magnificent cooked in this way – especially those large, firm plums that appear towards the end of summer – ones that split easily and pull away from their seeds. To make sugar-glazed plums, take one of these, split it, and place both sides, cut surfaces down, on a hot grill for a couple of minutes. Then, turn them through 90 degrees and cook for a couple more minutes. Lift them off the grill and place, cut sides up, in foil halos like the ones we used for the apples and pears.

Sprinkle the char-grilled surfaces with a raw, pure sugar and return them to the grill to roast until the fruit softens. Lift off and place each in a bowl, top with honey-sweetened natural yoghurt and sprinkle with unsalted, roasted almonds. The cheeks of mangoes, treated the same as the halved plums, are brilliant, too.

PINEAPPLE WEDGES: sweet and smoked

American barbecue guru Steven Raichlen, a good friend, showed me a way to roast whole, peeled pineapples on a rotisserie and sprinkle them with cinnamon sugar as they cook, and it was delicious with vanilla ice-cream.

FRESH PINEAPPLE

FRESH LIME JUICE

PALM SUGAR

VANILLA ICE-CREAM

FRESH MINT

But personally, I find a gentle Asian twist makes for a more interesting dish, so try my sweet pineapple wedges – a brilliant thing to do with a fresh, sweet pineapple.

Peel the pineapple and split it into quarters, vertically. Slice the sharp, central edge from each quarter, removing the core. Slice each quarter into two, lengthways, creating small wedges.

Soak these in a generous mixture of freshly squeezed lime juice into which you have grated plenty of palm sugar – for 6 limes, at least a couple of those knobs in which the sugar usually comes, or as much as you can work into the juice. Soak them overnight in the fridge if you like, or at least for several hours.

Grill these little boats on a hot gas grill, a Weber kettle or a Big Green Egg, following the 45-degree through 90-degree technique, which you should be able to do in your sleep by now, to impart a lattice of grill marks. Give them at least 2 minutes in each position.

Serve them on platters as finger food or, more formally, on small plates, each accompanied by a globe of good vanilla ice-cream, a drizzle of the lime syrup in which they soaked and a sprig of fresh mint.

Simple, delicious and a great thing to eat as the smoke of the day's barbecuing begins to disperse, and your neighbours, who were not invited but involuntarily shared the aromas, give some serious thought as to whether or not they will speak to you, ever again.

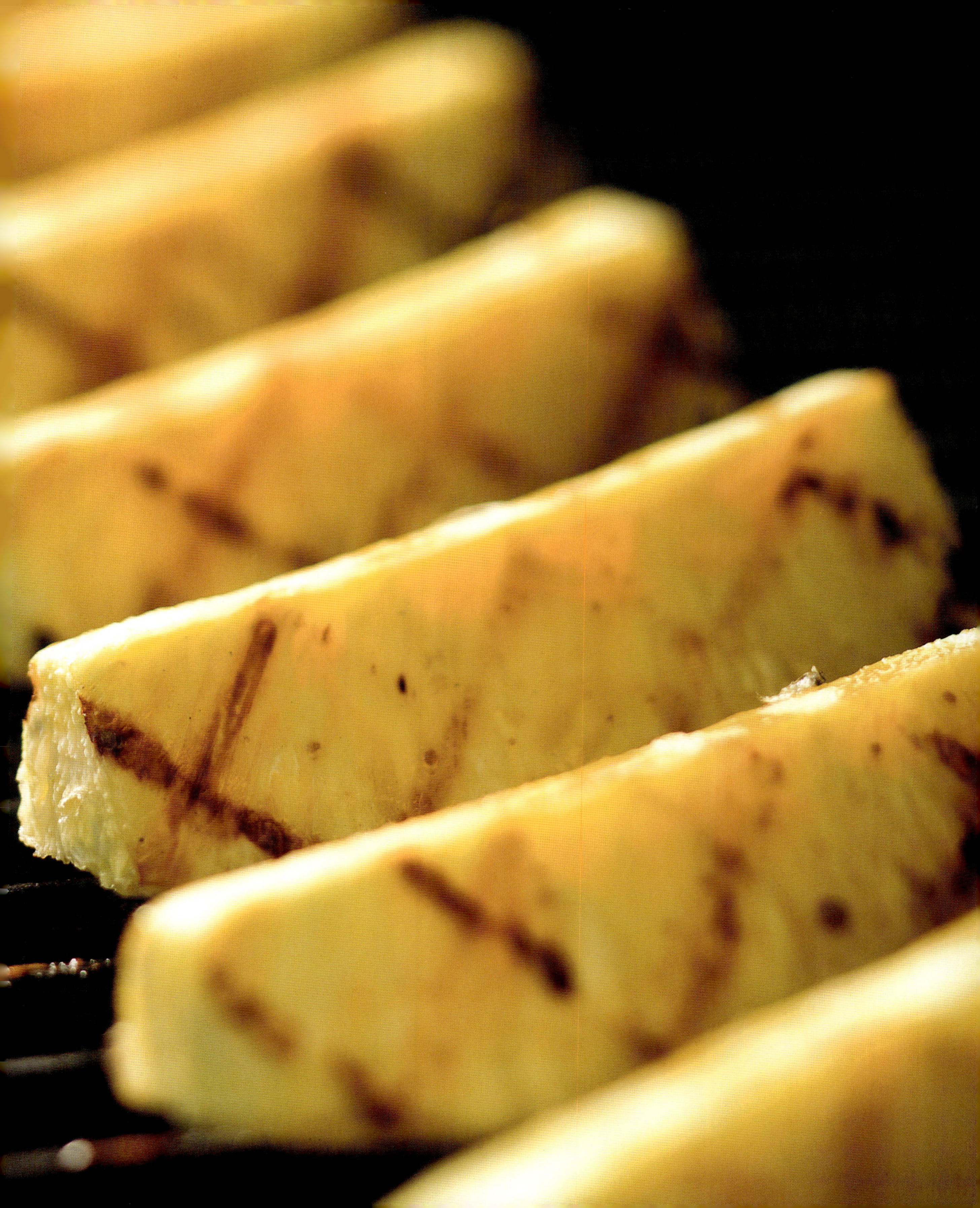

ONE LAST THING: do your kids smoke?

Outdoor occasions on which food is grilled, roasted or smoked on a barbecue can be very special family affairs – occasions that kids will remember, and treasure in later life. Even if they are remembered for the appalling food Dad offered around – years before he was given a copy of this book, of course.

But to make it really special, why not involve kids in the barbecue process, show them what you are up to, and let them play a part? The enthusiasm of many kids for food preparation clearly stems from the huge popularity of TV's *MasterChef*, so take full advantage of it.

Tongs are safe and simple implements, even for kids, provided a mitt or gauntlet is worn. Show kids how soon they should turn things like lamb cutlets, and how long they should leave a slab of fish in peace, if they want to impress the judges.

But if they are not quite ready for that, invest in a toasting fork and a bag of giant American marshmallows, probably from USA Foods in Moorabbin. Getting toasted marshmallows just right, by rotating them over the charcoal when the serious cooking is done, is an art form. Ask any kid.

Can you get them evenly charred and soft in the middle without their dropping off the fork and into the fire? Let the kids take a shot at it, learn to blow out the flame when their marshmallow catches, and also learn when not to put the molten marshmallow into their mouths.

In the process, they will learn something about the glorious process of barbecue. And may well pick up additional information of value. Such as what sort of knot to tie in the rope that attaches the hotplate, the one with the hole in the corner, to their rowing boat, serving a useful purpose for once – as an anchor.

Now, would the last one out please close the vents on the Weber kettle and the Big Green Egg, and turn off the gas.

Cheers...

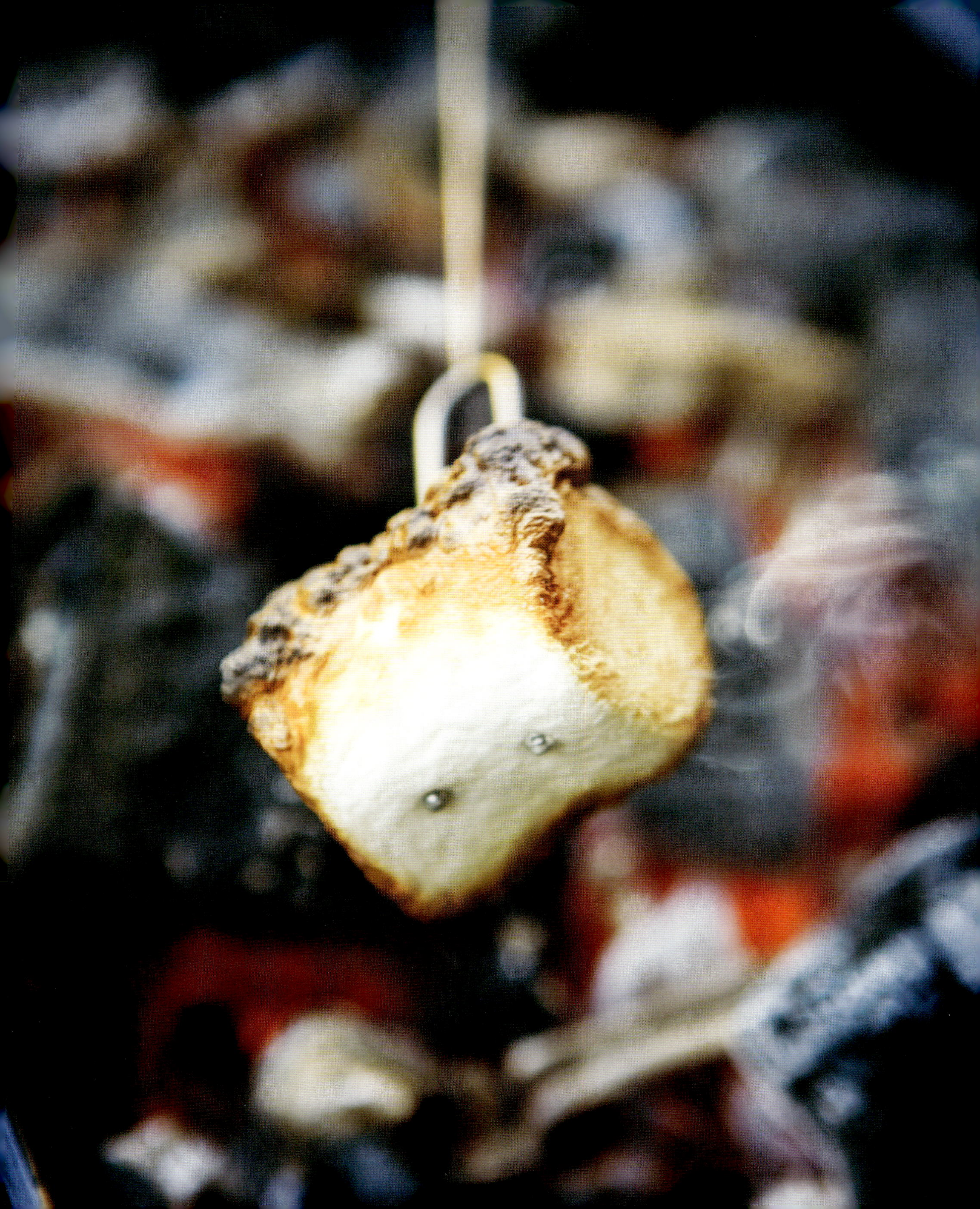

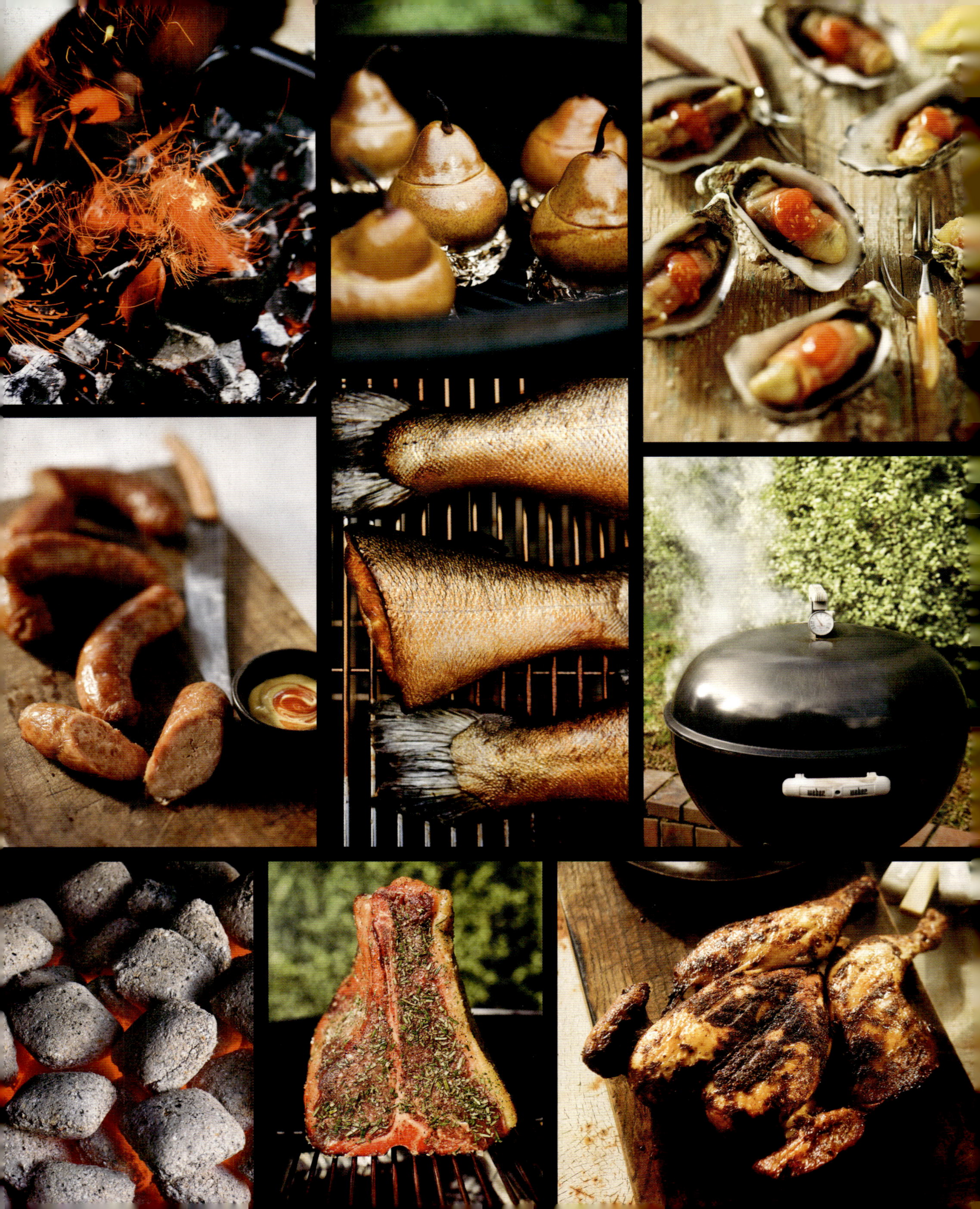

ACKNOWLEDGEMENTS

All the smoke in the world could not conceal the magnificent support we have received in the production of this book.

In addition to guidance and technical support from the incomparable team at Weber (Australia), especially from Dave Burden, and a never-ending supply of briquettes from the miracle workers at Heat Beads, we have been provided with the best and freshest fruit and vegetables by Toscano's of Kew, the legendary Melbourne green grocers. Our thanks, especially, to Joe, Pat, Dominic and Damian.

And when it came to washing down the food we prepared, we did so in wondrous style with the brilliant wines that carry the Ladies who Shoot their Lunch label from Plunkett Fowles in the Strathbogie Ranges of Victoria, especially the glorious shiraz, but also the wild-ferment chardonnay and the riesling. Superb.

We are fanatical about the meat we use. Because of that, we have cooked with only the finest money can buy – from Jonathan's of Collingwood and Donati's Fine Meats of Lygon St, Carlton. Game birds and poultry, including quail, spatchcock and corn-fed chickens, came from Game Farm of New South Wales, and were of exemplary quality.

Our salmon and baby salmon came from New Zealand King Salmon, who fly fresh fish from their Nelson salmon farms into Melbourne three times a week, and the rest of our seafood came from Ocean Made of Robert Street, Collingwood, and Canals Seafoods of Nicholson Street, Carlton North.

We also received invaluable support from Monterey Foods in Sydney, whose on-line service and range of Mexican foods is remarkable, and who understand the importance of chipotle, food of the gods. Also, our thanks to the outstanding USA Foods of Moorabbin, who sell cool stuff nobody even knows about. Except for us. And now, you.

And finally, my thanks to Steven Raichlen, US barbecue guru extraordinaire, a good friend and a top bloke. Nobody does it better.

SEEING THROUGH THE SMOKE

AN INDEX

a
adobo **12, 14, 104**
apples, mars bar **113**
artichokes, globe **106**
asparagus **98**

b
barbecue, definition **1**
barbecue sauce, all-purpose **14**
beef **55-67**
    brisket **58**
    ribs **56, 60**
    bone marrow **66**
butter, compound **12**

c
calamari **37**
cedar, planks & shingles **42**
charcoal **2-4, 7-8**
cheese starter **20**
chicken **86-93**
    Beer-butt chook **88**
    butterfly **92**
chilli **12, 14, 16, 17, 23, 24, 100, 104**
chimichurri **12**
chipotle **11, 12, 14, 24, 83, 98, 100**
corn **23, 97, 98, 100**
crème fraîche **47, 50, 56, 60, 110**

d
dill **12, 41, 42, 44, 51**
duck, grilled breasts **94**

f
firelighters **4**
fruit **108-115**

h
halloumi **23**
hickory **1, 2, 7, 12, 18, 29, 32, 34, 39, 44, 47, 49, 52, 56, 58, 60, 68, 74, 78, 80, 88, 92, 94, 104, 110, 113**
horseradish **30, 47, 51, 56, 58, 60**
hotplates **4-5, 78, 116**

j
jalapeño poppers **24**

k
kilpatrick sauce **30**

l
lamb **80-85**
    butterflied leg **80**
    cutlets **83**
    riblets **84**
lime **37, 114**
moscato **18**

m

marshmallows 116
mayonnaise 14, 51, 52, 100, 102
mint 12, 16, 18, 114
mint pesto 12, 83
mitts 7
mop sauce 11, 12, 17, 58, 71
mushrooms 102-104
mussels, grilled 32

o

onions, red, stuffed, roasted 104
oysters 29-30

r

ribs, see: beef, lamb, pork
rubs 11, 60, 63, 71, 74, 88, 92

s

salmon 41-47, 51
salsa verde 16
sausages 78
seafood 27
squire (aka pinkies) 37
steak 63-67
    entrecôte (porterhouse, sirloin) 66
    rib eye 63
spare ribs (pork) 74-77

p

pears, asian roasted 110
parsley 12, 16, 23, 32, 86, 102, 104
pickles, kosher dill 51
pineapple 114
pinkies (aka squire) 37
pork 68-77
    cutlets 72
    pulled 71
    spare ribs 75-77
prawns, king or tiger 34
prosciutto 29, 34

t

texans 2, 58, 60
texas crutch 60, 71, 74
thermometers 7
tongs 7
trout 49-50
tuna 52

v, w

vegetables 96-107
vine clippings 2, 66
vinegar sauce, north carolina 16
weber 2, 5, 119

HEAT & SMOKE

Conceived and produced by Hartbeat Media
Title, text, design and concept: © Hartbeat Media 2011
Photographs: © Dean Cambray 2011
First published December 2011; reprinted May 2012 with a hint of fresh smoke.
All rights reserved
Endorsed by the Australian Barbecue Academy
(australianbarbecueacademy.com)

National Library of Australia Cataloguing-in-Publication entry
Hart, Bob.
Heat & Smoke / Bob Hart ; Dean Cambray.
ISBN: 9780646565521 (pbk.)
Subjects: Outdoor cooking - Australia; Barbecues (Fireplaces); Barbecuing.
Other Authors/Contributors: Cambray, Dean
Dewey number: 641.5784

Printed in China by The Australian Book Connection

Distributed in Australia by Peribo Pty Limited,
Ph: (02) 9457 0011 or info@peribo.com.au

Food preparation and recipes: Bob Hart
Photography and styling: Dean Cambray
Design and spiritual guidance: Dot Alcaide
Editing and sly commentary: Richard Conrad
Production and fashion advice: Keith Downes
Grill wrangler: Andrew Richardson
Finished dishes eaten by all of the above
Bones chewed by Bart

All rights reserved. No part of this publication may be reproduced, stored in a retrieval system, transmitted in any form or by any means, electronic, mechanical, photocopying, recording or otherwise, without the prior written permission of the publisher.

DISCLAIMER: While all due care has been taken in the development of the recipes and in the advice offered herein, any and all burns, serious injuries and/or deaths caused by following said advice is down to you, not us. So lift your game. No Texans, vegetarians or vegans were harmed in the creation of this work, but any number of tasty critters, large and small, were dispatched with ruthless efficiency. *So get over it.*

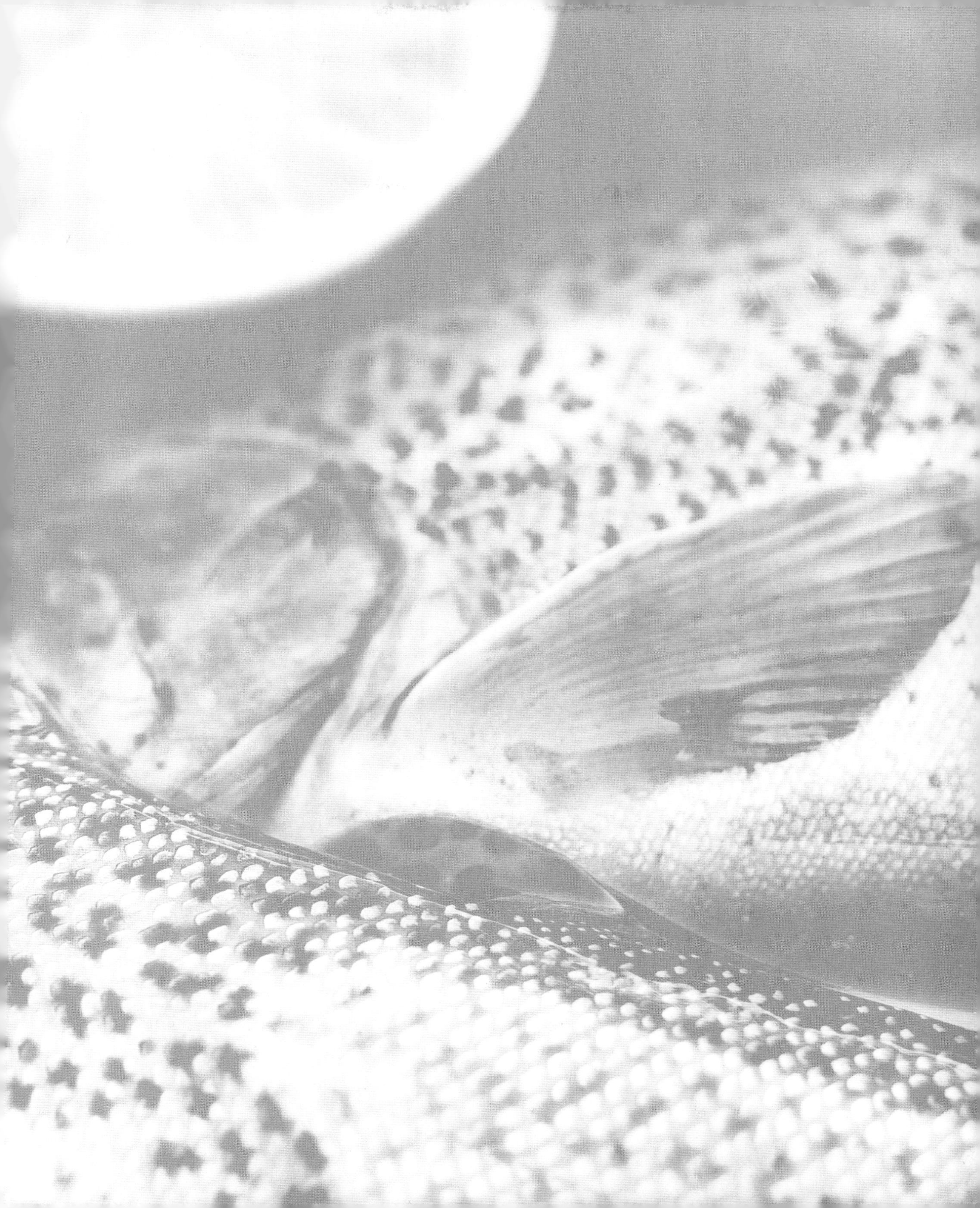

BOB HART

is an all-round food tragic who has become a Melbourne institution through his witty but authoritative writing and broadcasting on food over two decades. He trained, in Queensland, as a journalist and spent a decade writing first news, and then features and showbiz columns, for *The Sun* newspaper on London's Fleet Street in the golden era of newspapers. He then worked in the record industry, mining another golden era, before returning to journalism in general, and food writing in particular, in Melbourne in the early 1990s. His passion for barbecue began in the years he lived in the US where, in 1980, he bought his first Weber kettle. And the smoke began to rise…

Picture by Shannon Morris

DEAN CAMBRAY

is a larger-than-life culinary and photographic genius who has always been driven by his love for food: he trained and triumphed as a chef in some of Europe's finest kitchens, shone as a restaurateur with his Melbourne restaurant, Cambray's, which earned three hats in *The Age Good Food Guide*, and then refocussed his passion by picking up a camera, retraining as a photographer, and quickly becoming one of Australia's top food shooters. He has shot books, TV series stills, ad campaigns here and in the US, and, famously, partnered Bob Hart in their celebrated Saturday restaurant pages in the *Weekend* magazine of Melbourne's *Herald Sun*.

Picture by Suzette Nesire

NOTE: Neither Bob Hart nor Dean Cambray are vegans, vegetarians or thin. Dean likes to cycle vast distances, Bob likes to fly-fish for trout and, between them, they have eaten more glorious food than most medium-sized towns.